Teenage
Runaway

By John Benton

Teenage Runaway

━━❄️❄️ by John Benton ❄️❄️━━

SPIRE 🕊️ BOOKS

Fleming H. Revell Company
Old Tappan, New Jersey

Scripture quotations identified RSV are from the Revised Standard Version of the Bible, copyrighted 1946, 1952,© 1971 and 1973.

Library of Congress Cataloging in Publication Data

Benton, John, date
    Teenage runaway.

    I. Title.
PZ4.B4788Te   [PS3552.E57]   813   76-12603

A Spire Book ISBN 0-8007-8309-3

To
my wife, Elsie,
whose heart is always big
enough for all of the teenage runaways of this world

Teenage Runaway

1

I lay sprawled out on my bed, hands behind my head, gazing dreamily at the mirror on the opposite wall. I was alone in the house, able to relax and let my mind just wander.

I thought of Betty and Kathleen, former classmates of mine who had just had babies. Betty and her husband were living with his folks; Kathleen and hers had a tiny apartment and both parents were helping them out. Now, I was going to have a baby, and so far, it was my secret alone —no one else knew.

My stomach and my mind both churned. I felt proud, but rather scared, too, at the thought of becoming a mother. Would mine be the third shotgun wedding of the class? How would Danny feel? What would he say?

I grabbed the phone and dialed his number; suddenly I wanted to tell him the news so badly that I could hardly think.

"Hello," I heard him say.

"Guess what, Danny! I'm pregnant; you're going to be a father!" I blurted out.

"You're what?"

"Pregnant," I repeated, and laughed. "Congratulations, Daddy. When are we going to get married?"

"What?" he said again.

"Danny," I started. "I've got big news—"

There was a click, and the phone went dead.

I stared at the receiver and finally hung up slowly. I was crushed; I had never pictured *this* reaction. A tear or two trickled down my cheek and I was ready to really bawl, until I realized how startled Danny must have been.

Then I began to rationalize—to make excuses for him. After all, Betty and Kathleen had been going steady for almost a year; Danny and I had had only a few dates. Also, he had told me he was a virgin—come to think of it, I had never bothered to tell him I was, too. I decided I would try him again, and this time I'd be more tactful.

I dialed him right back before I lost my nerve.

His mother answered the phone. I used my sweetest voice. "Mrs. Vaughan, this is Becky. Is Danny there?"

"Why, I think so. Weren't you just talking to him?" She sounded surprised. "Is something the matter?"

"Uh . . . uh . . . no, we just had a little misunderstanding and I want to straighten things out," I said.

"Well, let me see if he's still around," she said. There was a long pause and then Danny came on.

"Danny, I'm sorry I surprised you so, but I just figured with us so much in love and all, that you'd be as excited as I am. Danny, please don't be so cold. We've got to get together and figure out what to do," I pleaded.

"Listen, Becky, I know I did wrong," he said. "And I'm sorry. Don't you remember I told you I was sorry?"

I was beginning to get a little mad. "Yes, Daddy, I remember," I said sarcastically.

"Don't you ever call me 'Daddy' again," he snarled. "You're not going to pin this rap on me. So far as I'm concerned you can go out and hunt yourself up another daddy—there were probably plenty of others."

Bang went the phone again and, again, I was holding a dead receiver. I was good and mad by now and my only thoughts were how I could get back at Danny.

Before long, my senses returned and I realized I would have to talk to someone—a person with more experience than I had—to figure out how to deal with Danny and what we should do. But who? My mother? She was handy; she was older; she had more experience. Yes, but—so far, what help had she been with my other problems? None!

Finally, I hit on Nordine. Nordine was twenty, but she was a good friend and, most important, she was compassionate and understanding. Yes, Nordine would advise me what to do, I decided.

After supper, I walked over to Nordine's apartment. Her friend Lucy, a nurse at Arden Hospital, was already there when I arrived.

I felt that I had really lucked out. I didn't know Lucy very well, but I liked her; now, I had two older girls to talk to, and one of them a nurse, to boot.

After we exchanged greetings, I sat down on the sofa and blurted out my news: "I've got something to tell you. I'm going to have a baby."

"Well, welcome to the club," Lucy said, after a minute. "You must make number 1,676,329. Getting pregnant is the *in* thing these days."

"Don't be flip," Nordine snapped. She reached over and took my hand. "Becky is in trouble and she needs help, not wisecracks."

I looked at the two older girls helplessly. "What do you suggest?" I asked. "Danny won't admit it is his."

"Want to know something, Becky?" Lucy asked slowly.

"What do you mean do I want to know something? I'm in trouble, you smart aleck. Have you got all the answers for a girl who's been knocked up?"

"Some," she replied shortly. "I had an abortion."

Nordine and I stared at her. Finally, Nordine spoke up.

"Lucy, I can't believe a good Christian girl like you would ever have an abortion."

"Well, I did. I won't bother with all the details. It was the same old story: a good-looking guy told me he loved me and he convinced me there was nothing wrong in going to bed with him. Of course, as soon as I got pregnant, he dumped me.

"I thought about nothing else for weeks. I talked to other nurses; I talked to doctors I knew. I even prayed."

"Do you mean to tell me," I interrupted, "that after you prayed, you still decided to go ahead with an abortion?"

"Yes. There's a Scripture in the Bible that says something about laying your treasure up in heaven and not on earth. If I had that baby, I would certainly keep it on earth and who knows what would happen to it? When it grew up and died it might wind up in hell. But, if I had an abortion, that baby would go to heaven—even Jesus said that children would be in heaven. So I got the abortion," she finished.

"Are you sorry?" I asked.

"No."

"Do you mean you think that I should get an abortion? Even God would want me to get an abortion?"

"Well, you asked me; and that's the way I feel about it," Lucy said. "The important thing, though, is to go to a good hospital, have a good doctor. Don't let anyone sell you a bill of goods on self-aborting or taking a chance on some fly-by-night, or you're liable to wind up dead.

"Go to a Planned Parenthood agency and get the name of a good doctor. And go soon. It's very simple and it didn't hurt me a bit."

Nordine looked flabbergasted. She didn't say anything, just kept patting my shoulder, so, in a few minutes, I got up, thanked them both, and went on home.

I thought all the next day while my mother was at work, and by the time she came home, I knew I had to discuss the whole thing with her. I was only sixteen; I couldn't handle this all alone.

As she came in the back door, I greeted her. "Hi, Mom, I've got something important to discuss with you. Have you got a few minutes?"

"Hi, darling. Of course I have—always. Be with you in a minute."

She laid her purse on the dining-room table and walked on into the next room.

"Please sit here on the sofa with me," I said. I wasn't sure what her reaction would be when she found out her only child was pregnant. Would she faint? Or would she be matter-of-fact, as usual, and brush it aside?

"Well, what's the big news?" she asked as she seated herself.

"Mom, I'm pregnant."

The smile disappeared. She looked straight into my eyes, but didn't say a word.

My words tripped over each other in the rush to get them out. "It wasn't my fault. Danny Vaughan . . . he's the father . . . and he won't admit it. . . . "

I waited, I don't know for what—hopefully, a warm embrace, a long talk, maybe tears?

Instead, Mom got to her feet slowly. She looked at me —through me, almost—then turned and walked to her bedroom.

"Aren't you going to say something—anything?" I screamed. "Don't just walk away. Don't you understand what I just said? I'm going to have a baby. You're going to be a grandmother."

She didn't turn around, just walked into her room and closed the door.

I threw myself face down on the sofa and sobbed like a baby. I was sixteen; I was an adult; I was pregnant. I felt about six.

The following evening I decided to tackle Mom again. I had no idea whether she was hurt, stunned, or just noncommital as usual, and I was scared to probe. I really didn't want to know.

When she came home from work, I faced her. "Mom, I want an abortion."

"Whatever you say," she replied.

"Will you help me to go to the agency and see about getting one?" I asked hesitantly. "I'm not sure just what to do."

"Of course," she said. "But don't you think you should wait a bit and be sure? Maybe you really aren't pregnant. Did you miss your period?"

"I'm late. I mean, yes, I did," I stammered. "I *know* I'm pregnant."

"Well, let's wait a little longer. If you're pregnant, you're pregnant. If you really are, and still want an abortion, we'll go ahead. It won't really make that much difference," she said.

Reluctantly, I agreed. I remembered Lucy's warning words about going soon, but there was little else I could do if I wanted her help.

I was pretty miserable the next few weeks, both physically and mentally. When I began to have morning sickness I went to my mother again.

"No more waiting," I said firmly. "I know for sure now, and I want an abortion."

Mom agreed and called Planned Parenthood for an appointment three days later. As we got into the elevator I had the creepy feeling that everyone was looking at me and that they all knew I was pregnant. I kept my eyes glued to the floor until we reached the clinic.

The waiting room was full of girls. The woman at the reception desk took our names, asked us to sit down, and said the doctor would see us shortly.

I continued to stare at the floor, but no one said a word, so I finally sneaked a look at a girl across the room. Our eyes met, and we both glanced away quickly. I was scared to death and my heart was pounding.

The girl next to me began to twitch her fingers restlessly. I glanced over quickly and saw that she was fiddling with an engagement ring: her other hand was clasped firmly by a boy on her other side. What was he doing here —and why the ring?

I had to know, so I leaned over and whispered, "What's that ring doing on your finger?"

"George and I are going to get married in just five months," she replied. "Isn't that right, George?"

"That's right," he said, and grinned.

"Well, what are you doing here, then?" I asked.

"Same thing as you, I imagine," she said. "What are you here for?"

"I want an abortion," I whispered.

"Well, so do I," she said, and turned again to George.

My consternation must have shown on my face; several girls across the room must have heard our conversation— their expressions were astonished, too. A fiancé willing to come and hold your hand and *still* get an abortion—it was too much for me to comprehend.

Just then the nurse called us into the doctor's office. I

got up on the table, where he poked and prodded me.

"Yes, you're going to have a baby," he said. "Offhand, I'd say you're about twelve weeks along. You may have to go to a hospital if you wait much longer—only for a few days, though. The longer it is delayed the bigger the possibility of problems, so it's safer to go to the hospital."

I swung my legs over the side of the table. This doctor was crazy! I *knew* I couldn't be more than eight or nine weeks pregnant at most, and I wasn't about to go to any hospital.

"Listen, doctor," I said as I fumbled into my clothes. "You've done your part, now I'll do mine, and I'm not going to any hospital; I'm going home right now."

"Hold it," he replied. "Let's not get huffy and make a rash decision. I am going to give you the names of two excellent physicians who will go over you more thoroughly and decide just what steps need to be taken. It may be that you will not have to go to a hospital at all, but do go to one of them and go promptly."

The doctor handed Mom a slip of paper, which she stuck in her purse as we walked out.

The following morning at breakfast Mom suggested that I talk to our pastor. I respected the Reverend Hunter. He was a friendly man, with a good sense of humor, and he preached a good sermon, even though I didn't always practice what he advised. Mom's idea sounded like a good one so I agreed.

We went that very evening and he welcomed us warmly as he ushered us into his study. Mom and I sat together on the sofa, and he dropped into a nearby chair.

"Becky, your mother has already told me what has happened. There is no sense in my upbraiding you for doing wrong, so let's just go on from here."

"Did wrong?" I asked. "Danny said he loved me and I know I loved him, so it seemed right to us. The only thing wrong is that I got pregnant."

Mom interrupted before I could say more. "Now, Becky, listen to what Pastor Hunter has to say before you make any judgments. You believe in God, don't you? He is a man of God and will give you good advice."

She was right—I did believe in God. "Okay, Pastor, throw it at me," I grinned at him.

"My recommendation, Becky, is that you give the baby up for adoption," he said.

"You mean let someone else raise my child? And never know whether it goes to heaven or hell? You're crazy." My thoughts flew back to Lucy's advice from the Bible, but before I could go on, my mother broke in.

"Now, Becky, calm down. This is the best thing—for the baby, for you, for me, for our family, for the pastor, for the church," she said.

It was obvious that Mom and the pastor had decided this before hand, but I wasn't about to change my mind: I was going to have an abortion. I stood up, but before I could get to the door, the pastor picked up a Bible from the nearby desk and started to thumb through it.

"Becky," he said, "I'd like to talk to you as a friend—maybe even more than that, as a father to his daughter."

"As a friend, okay," I snapped. "But no father-daughter stuff—I hate my old man."

"Do you know what God says about abortion, Becky?" he asked. "You have your opinion, your mother may have hers, I may have mine, but won't you listen to God's?"

Again I thought of Lucy, so I said, "All right, go ahead. I've gotten just about everyone else's; I might as well get His."

"In the Book of Psalms He says, 'Thy eyes beheld my unformed substance; in thy book were written, every one of them, the days that were formed for me, when as yet there was none of them'" (139:16 RSV). He paused for a moment, then asked, "Do you know what that means?"

I was trying to puzzle it out but couldn't, so I said, "No."

"Even when we are in our formative stages in our mothers' wombs, God has plans for our lives. Anyone who aborts a pregnancy aborts God's plans and thus ends His plans for that yet unformed child."

"You mean God has plans even for this baby inside of me?"

"He sure does," he said firmly. "Wonderful plans, I might add."

I sat back and thought about that. I didn't always obey the Bible, but I believed in it, and I believed in God. Did I want to stand in God's way?

"What do you think, Mother?" I asked.

"The pastor is right. I was so sorry and guilt-ridden when I had my . . . ." Mom's voice trailed off in mid-sentence.

I stared at her unbelievingly. Was it possible that my own mother had had an abortion?

"You had your what?" I asked. But I got no answer. Mom stared at her feet, her face beet-red. The pastor shifted uneasily back and forth in his chair and eyed his feet, also. A big tear ran down my mother's cheek and splashed onto her dress; more followed.

"Mother, were you going to say that you had an abortion?" I asked bluntly. I *had* to have an answer.

Mom was really sobbing by this time and it was hard to understand the words that poured out of her. "Yes,

Becky, I did have an abortion, and I've been sorry ever since. When you announced the other day that you were pregnant, my past all came back in a rush. When I was barely seventeen an older man got me into trouble. He was married; he had a lot of excuses.

"I had no one to turn to. We didn't go to church. My mother was ashamed of me, so was my whole family. Someone told me about a woman who did abortions and I went to her. She lived in a filthy place and I almost died of infection, but I knew nothing else to do. There isn't a day I haven't been sorry," she said.

Pastor Hunter handed her a tissue, but she continued to sob hysterically. He rose and put his hand on her shoulder. "Mrs. Swenson," he said, "when you asked Jesus to forgive you your sins, He did just that. His blood has wiped out your past; it's as though it never happened. He doesn't want any of us to live under a burden of guilt and sin. Jesus has come to lift our burden."

"Jesus has come to lift our burden." It sounded wonderful. Only He could lift mine. My eyes got hot, and tears started to run down my cheeks. I dabbed at them and looked at the pastor—he was crying, too!

I slid over and put my arm around Mom to comfort her. Her crying stopped and she, in turn, put her arm around me and drew me close. It felt wonderful; she had never shown that kind of love for me before. I was at peace.

The pastor coughed. "To get back to the main problem: I will see what I can do about getting Becky into a home for unwed mothers in Saint Louis. The girls stay in the home until they have their babies and then the home places them with good families. It is probably too late tonight, but I'll call first thing in the morning," he ended.

"Okay, Pastor, go ahead," I said.

"You're doing the right thing, Becky," Mother said, and hugged me.

I really felt good. It was the first time in a long while that my mother had told me I was doing the right thing. There was just one thing that hung in the back of my mind as we started to leave.

"Pastor, can you answer one question for me?" I asked.

"I guess so. What's on your mind?"

"Do you think people who have abortions are murderers?"

His face went blank. "What do you think, Becky?"

"I don't know," I replied. "That's why I'm asking you."

Mom grabbed my arm and pushed me out of the door before he could reply. "We'll expect to hear from you tomorrow," she said.

The phone call came through: I was to leave for Saint Louis the next day, by plane. On the spur of the moment, I decided to call Danny and tell him the news.

"Oh, Becky, I am glad to hear that," he said. "I'm sure everything is going to turn out all right for us."

"What do you mean 'for us'?" I was flabbergasted.

"I've thought and thought about what's happened. Half a dozen times I've started to call, but somehow I never had the nerve. I'm sorry I reacted the way I did; I guess I am the father and probably the best thing for us to do is get married. Don't you think so?" The words came out in a rush; I could tell they had been bottled up for a long time.

But why was Danny changing his mind, especially now that other plans were shaping up? Did he really love me, or did he only feel sorry for me? I had to know.

"Danny, how much do you really love me?"

"More than this world," he said fervently.

"Would you still love me—and marry me—if I got an abortion?"

There was a long pause. "Say, that sounds like a good idea," he said.

"That's not what I asked you. Would you still love me if I got an abortion?"

"Say, I know a fellow whose girl got an abortion and no one knew a thing about it, only took a few minutes, too. You want me to get more information?" He sounded enthusiastic.

Danny's attitude was like that of so many others I'd talked to—a simple solution to a simple problem: get pregnant, get an abortion. But I felt differently now—I wasn't going to stand in God's way or spoil His plans for this baby.

"Well, Danny, I am still going out to Saint Louis tomorrow. I still love you, but I have decided abortion is wrong," I said.

"Okay," he said. "You do what you think is best. Abortion sounds like a good idea to me, but it's your decision. Just remember I have changed my mind and we can always get married."

When he offered to take me to the airport the next day, I felt a lot better. He sounded more like the old Danny, and maybe he really did care.

My stay in Saint Louis was short and almost a disaster. I had convinced myself that the long months there wouldn't be so bad, as there would be a lot of other girls at the home to talk to, and we all had a common problem. But it didn't turn out that way.

A woman from the home met me and explained that the home was full, but she was placing me in a good, kind, Christian home. The woman and three kids weren't bad at all, but the husband was something else. He quoted the

Bible constantly—mostly about sinners—and expected me to shoot back Bible quotations.

I was so homesick I called my mother every day. She urged me to stick it out. I called Danny a few times, too, and each time he repeated that we could get married. In my state, it wasn't hard to convince myself that he really loved me.

I called my mother once more and told her I wanted to come home. I told her Danny and I were going to get married, but she would have no part of it. She said Danny was irresponsible, had no job, could not possibly be a husband, and would certainly fail as a father. When I told her Danny's parents had said we could live with them, she just laughed.

That night, when the man of the house baited me again, I ran to a phone booth and called Danny. He said he would send me the airfare to get home and would meet me at the airport. I was so desperate I was sure Mom wouldn't turn me away; I remembered that night in the pastor's study so vividly.

When Danny delivered me to my door, Mom took one look at me and screamed, "I'll have no part of this. Danny Vaughan, I can have you arrested. My daughter is under-age. You had no business bringing her back."

I was tired from the trip and more than upset at her reaction, so I lashed out at her, "Danny and I are going to get married. And if you don't give us permission, I'll broadcast my pregnancy from the rooftops. I could care less what the community thinks, but you do care, and *you* will be the one to be disgraced."

Her face fell. "All right," she said, "come in."

The next day, Danny and I went to Pastor Hunter to see about getting married, but I soon realized that Mom had already spoken to him. He acted surprised to see me back, but he did his utmost to talk Danny and me out of marriage: We were too young; Danny had no job; I was irresponsible. Finally, he flatly refused to officiate at our wedding. He asked me to pray about it!

We left and on the way home, Danny said we could try his minister. He didn't sound very enthusiastic, but I was determined to get married.

When I walked into the house, Mom was sitting at the kitchen table, just staring at the wall. Her eyes were red and when she spoke, it was obvious she'd been crying.

"Becky," she said, "I've been doing a lot of thinking. I know exactly what will happen if you and Danny get married. You are both way too young. You'll get married; you'll have the baby. At first it will be fun, and then the next thing you know you and Danny will be getting a divorce. And who will wind up with the baby? Me!"

Well, I thought, here it comes; back to Saint Louis.

But Mom went on. "I've wrestled with this problem and finally have to admit that you are right; you should get an abortion. Grandma has agreed to pay for it."

I couldn't believe my ears. After her confession in the pastor's study, it was impossible that she would want me to suffer the guilt feelings she had had.

"But Mom," I protested, "there must be some reason. Tell me honestly, why have you done such an about-face?"

She looked at me a little shamefaced, but finally said, "Well, if you really want to know the truth, I don't think I could stand the disgrace of having people know my daughter *had* to get married. Can you understand that?"

Well, no, I really couldn't understand it. It was *my* life, not hers. But what kid can figure out what really bugs his parents?

Before I could get my wits about me, Mom started to cry again. She put her arms around me and said she would make all the arrangements and she would see me through the worst of it.

I thought of Danny; he wanted an abortion, too. It seemed the pastor and I were a minority. I didn't understand much of it, but it was warming to have Mom love me again, so I agreed.

The next day, we headed into Manhattan to one of the doctors who had been recommended to us. Grandma was with us, but no one said a word.

Finally, I asked the question that had been bothering me ever since the day before. "Mother, you mentioned in the pastor's office the great burden of guilt you carried. What about me? How am I going to handle that?"

Mom stared at the road ahead and didn't say a word. The traffic was pretty heavy, so I decided I'd better shut up, or we might all wind up dead.

But what about *my* guilt? And what was God going to think of all this?

The doctor and nurse were very kind. When he first came in, I was uptight and acted pretty rude.

"Hello, Becky, how are you?" the doctor asked.

"Pregnant," I snapped. "I hope soon I won't be. . . . I'm sorry, I really didn't mean that. I feel fine."

"That's okay, Becky," he said. "It's natural that you're a bit edgy."

The doctor explained everything they were doing as he and the nurse worked together. Finally, he hooked up what he explained was a suction tube. I heard a whoosh of air and a gurgle in my stomach.

"Okay, that's it. You lie quietly for a few minutes," said the doctor as he left the room.

I looked at the nurse in amazement. "You mean that's all?" I asked.

"That's it," she replied. "You came in early enough. Now lie quietly, I'll be back in a few minutes."

After she left, I got a terrific impulse to look into the plastic bag they had used. I tried to sit up, but got so dizzy I had to lie down again. I was about to try again when the nurse came back, carried out the bag, and told me I could sit up for a while; she would be back.

When the nurse returned she helped me dress and walked me out to the waiting room. I shrugged off her hand and walked over to Mom and Grandma.

"Come on," I said. "It's all over."

When we got into the car, Grandma said the only words she uttered on the whole trip: "Don't tell anybody, and don't ever do this again or I'll disown you."

I looked over at Mother, but she didn't say a word, just kept her eyes on the road ahead. The rest of the trip was made in silence.

Mom insisted I lie down for a while when we got in. I was restless, but I agreed. I decided to call Danny—I had to talk to someone.

"Danny, I finally have some news that will make you happy," I said.

"What?"

"I got an abortion."

"That's terrific." He really sounded happy. "I suppose you are real glad it's over?"

Glad? Happy? I couldn't say I felt either: I felt let down. I knew Someone who wasn't happy—God.

"Well, what did you find out from your minister?" I asked. "When can we get married?"

"Married? What for?"

"But Danny," I stammered, "that's what you wanted. I got the abortion for you. . . . You said you loved me. . . . You wanted to marry me. . . . "

"I did what I had to, Becky; It's over now, done with. Do me a favor and don't call again."

My thoughts wouldn't come together; I felt numb all over. Here I had gotten an abortion to please my boyfriend —like the girl in the Planned Parenthood agency—and now I had no boyfriend. My mother and my grandmother were no help; I couldn't call on God.

The tears came finally, and I cried and cried until I fell asleep. When I awoke the following day, I felt heavy, as though I had not slept at all. A big, dark feeling was there —guilt.

No one had come near me in the hours I spent there in my room, and I knew at last that I had to get out of here. I had to get away from this place—this town—where no one cared. I would have to run away and see if I could make a new life.

2

I stood by the curb just a block from home, my heart beating so hard I felt it would burst out of my chest. It's one thing to leave your house forever, but it's something else again to try to get a ride away from your neighborhood where everyone knows you. I felt that the police would be after me any moment, or someone I knew would come along and see my little bag.

I decided I'd better get back on the sidewalk and walk until I got into a new area, so I picked up the flight bag and started off. Soon the sidewalks ended, and I decided it was time for me to try to thumb a ride. I heard a car approaching and stuck my whole hand out quickly.

An old couple slowed almost to a stop, then, as they drew abreast and looked me over, the car picked up speed again and on they went. What was the matter with me, I wondered. What had I done wrong?

I walked on again, stopping to stick out my thumb at each approaching car, but still no one stopped. It seemed like hours and I was getting discouraged, when I heard a car coming and decided to try again. Just in time, I realized the car heading toward mc was a state police car!

I panicked and plunged into the woods bordering the road. I ran until I could run no more. I sprawled on the ground, straining to listen for feet crashing through the brush. Had the cop seen me and stopped? Or had he gone on? I waited for about fifteen minutes, but all I could hear

was cars speeding by, so I got up slowly and walked warily
back to the road.

Just short of the road I dropped to my hands and knees
and crept through the brush until I could see the road in
both directions. I breathed a sigh of relief—no cars were
in sight.

I started to walk down the road again. At least if a cop
came by again, I would be walking, not hitchhiking. It was
beginning to get dark and I began to worry. I had never
given a thought to where I would spend the night. Where
do runaways put up at night?

I wanted to get as far away from home as I could, but
something had to happen fast—I knew I couldn't walk all
the way to the West Coast, and what about tonight?

I looked down the road and saw what looked like a van
approaching. Out went my thumb and on my face I put
the biggest smile I could muster. The van pulled over!

I ran up alongside and opened the door hopefully.

"Hello there," the driver said. "Hop in."

I scrambled in, slammed the door, and turned to get a
better look at the driver. He had long hair and a short
beard. He wasn't bad looking, and not too old.

"Sure appreciate your stopping for me," I said. "I
thought no one was ever going to pick me up."

"Oh, that's okay. I'm always glad to help out a runaway," the driver replied.

"What?"

"Come on, don't try fooling me. I know what you're up
to," he laughed.

How could this guy know I was running away? Certainly he didn't know me or my family. He didn't look like
a cop; he looked too with it for that. Yet, I had heard
about cops who dress up like hippies. I didn't know what
to do.

"Who are you, anyhow?" I asked.

"Art Koons," he said shortly. He kept his eyes on the road, but a smile lurked around his lips.

I decided to be quiet. If I talked, I might talk too much, and he might trap me into giving him more information than I wanted to give.

"What's your name?" he asked finally. "And never mind giving me a phony—I want your real name."

"Becky Swenson," I said. I was too scared to lie.

"How far are you going?" he asked.

I thought frantically. If I told him I wanted to go as far west as possible he'd know for sure I was a runaway, and then what would he do? Suddenly I thought of my aunt in Pittsburgh.

"I hope to get to Pittsburgh," I said. "I'm going out to my aunt's there. I'd planned to take the bus, but I'm saving my money for college, so I decided to see if I could hitch my way instead."

"Oh, I see. You have an aunt in Pittsburgh?

"Yes," I stammered. "Aunt . . . Aunt Mary. . . . "

"Aunt Mary, huh? And I suppose your uncle's name is John? John Doe, maybe?"

"No, no. My uncle's name is Frank. What makes you such a wise guy, anyway?" I asked.

He didn't say anything, just turned and gave me a little lopsided grin, before he returned his attention to driving. I put my head back on the seat and started to drowse, when I heard Art say, "Hey, look what's ahead—a couple of cop cars."

I almost jumped out of my skin. I stared ahead through the dark, and sure enough, just up ahead were two familiar-colored state police cars pulled up at the side of the road. My heart sank as Art lifted his foot from the accelerator.

"Guess I'll stop and ask how the weather is up ahead," he said.

"Oh, I wouldn't bother with that," I said hastily. "It's a beautiful night—looks even nicer up ahead. Please, just keep on going."

Frantically, I reached out and grabbed his arm.

"Hey, what's the matter with you?" he asked. "Want to have an accident?"

I didn't notice the little smile still on his lips; we were almost up to the police cars and I had to do something.

"Okay, I was lying," I screamed. "I'm a runaway, and you know it. But if the cops find out we'll both be in trouble. Please, please don't stop."

Immediately, the van picked up speed. In seconds we were past the police and driving on down the dark highway, still heading west.

I stared straight ahead. That was too close for comfort; my heart would not stop its deafening pounding. What did this goon want, anyway? He was beginning to scare me almost as much as the cops.

A guffaw broke the silence. I stared at Art in disbelief. How could he be laughing at a moment like this? The more I stared, the harder he laughed.

"Well, what's so darned funny?" I snapped at him.

"You," he said, wiping his eyes with the back of one hand. "You really fell for that little game I played with you. You never fooled me for a minute with that Pittsburgh-college-aunt jazz. I knew you were a runaway the minute I spotted you. And you really fell, hook, line, and sinker, for that gag about stopping to ask the cops about the weather!"

"Why, you dirty, stinking rat!" I was furious. How could he have scared me so just for a laugh?

"Okay, okay, calm down. You'll have to get used to my sense of humor if you're going to ride far with me," Art said. "And I just happen to have a little proposition that might interest you," he added.

I was wary. Was this another gag? "What's that?" I asked shortly.

"By a very strange coincidence I am heading for San Francisco," he said. "Want to ride along?"

"San Francisco! Sure do, that sounds terrific!"

"We have only one minor problem," Art said. "Money. I've only got twenty bucks. We can bunk in the back of the van, but twenty bucks isn't going to buy us food and gas to get to the Coast."

All I had was ten dollars of hard-earned baby-sitting money. I was afraid that wouldn't help much, but I decided to offer it to him.

I reached into my pocket, pulled out the bill, and started to hand it to Art, but then a thought hit me and I pulled my hand back quickly.

"This isn't a rip-off, is it?" I asked. "How do I know you won't just take my ten dollars and throw me out?"

Art laughed appreciatively. "You're learning, Becky, you're learning fast. But how are you going to get to the Coast if you don't hand it over?"

He had a point. His way was the easiest way for me to get to San Francisco, if I could trust him. I had little choice. Reluctantly, I handed him the bill.

He stuffed it into his jeans and laughed again. "Now, don't you worry, Becky. So long as you're my girl, I'm going to look after you—all the way to the Coast and in San Fran and L.A., too; I got connections there. I liked

your looks the minute I saw you, like your spunk, too.
You and I are going to make a good team, kiddo. Just
remember, I didn't turn you in to the cops, did I? Trust
me and everything will come up smelling like roses for
you."

I believed him. I *had* to believe him or I'd never make
it across the country. I gave him a small smile and
dropped my head back to take another snooze. All this
excitement had made me dead tired, and it was late. For
better or worse, I was in Art's hands.

The stopping of the van awakened me. I went to the
ladies' room while Art gassed up, and I returned to the
van in time to see him give the attendant my ten-dollar
bill. He picked up a handful of candy bars with the change
and we headed on down the highway.

We drove on to a truck stop and Art parked at the edge.
He opened the van door, then beckoned me to get into the
back.

"Here's where we stop for the rest of the night," he said.

It was just past daylight when Art wakened me and we
went into the diner and had a good breakfast. When Art
paid the bill, I noticed he had only five dollars left, but I
decided I'd better not say anything.

As we traveled down the highway, Art entertained me
with stories about the West Coast—especially about San
Fran and L.A. He assured me again that he'd take me all
the way and find us a place to stay after we got there. I
felt safe and protected for the first time in weeks, until I
remembered the five-dollar bill.

"Art, how are we going to get all the way to San Francisco on just five dollars?"

"Ever hear of Bonnie and Clyde?" he asked.

This guy really was a nut! Who hadn't heard of Bonnie and Clyde?

"What have Bonnie and Clyde got to do with us getting to the Coast?"

"See that gas station on up ahead?" he asked. "Well, I figure you and I ought to be able to pick up at least two hundred there and that ought to get us there comfortably."

I was getting aggravated. None of this conversation made sense to me.

"And just *how* are we going to get the money?" I asked. "Just walk in and ask the owner to help us out?"

Art's face was very serious as he replied. "Well, sort of. I'm all prepared. There are four guns in the back. You strap one on each side and I'll do the same. We'll just walk in there and ask the man to kindly give us the money."

My mouth flew open, but no words would come out. I finally stuttered, "But, suppose—suppose he doesn't?"

"Well, then, we just shoot him and take the money," Art answered matter-of-factly.

"But Art, I . . . I . . . I've never shot a gun. Besides, I'm just not the type—I know I could never go through with anything like that."

"Sure you can. Like I said, I admire your spunk," he replied as he started to slow down.

Visions of myself strapped into the electric chair ran through my head; of my mother writing a book about her famous daughter, the cold-blooded murderess. I started to bawl.

And Art started to laugh. Belatedly, I realized that once again he was playing games with me.

It took me a while to control my sobbing and feel my knees stop shaking. I was pretty mad: I didn't know how

I'd survive the trip if Art kept pulling stunts like this. His was a pretty perverted sense of humor, so far as I was concerned, and I told Art so.

"You're such an easy one to kid," he said. "I just can't help it." He was completely unrepentant. He reached over, patted my knee, and continued, "Well, since you won't be my gunman—pardon me, my gun moll—you just sit there and act as lookout for me. As soon as you see a hitchhiker, let me know and I'll take it from there."

"A hitchhiker? What good is a hitchhiker going to do us?" I didn't know if he was pulling a new gag or not.

"Never mind, you just keep your eyes peeled and sing out when you see one—either side of the road."

Dutifully, I glued my eyes to the road. Soon I saw a figure plodding along the side.

"Hey," I said to Art, "up ahead there, to the right. That guy is thumbing, isn't he?"

"Aha, that looks like a likely pigeon," Art. said. "Let's pick him up and see what develops."

Art pulled abreast of the fellow and he hopped in. He was about twenty. After Art introduced himself and me, the boy said his name was Ron and he was on his way to Ohio. He'd been visiting his parents in New York and was on his way back to school at Ohio State University. I smiled but didn't say anything, as I'd no idea what Art was going to do.

Art pulled his wallet out of his hip pocket and flipped it open to show the five. "I'll lay it on the line, Ron. You look like a nice guy, maybe you can help us out. That five bucks is all we have, and we're trying to get to California. We're just about out of gas. Do you think you could kick in a couple of bucks or so to help us on our way?"

"Why, sure," Ron said. "At least I can pay for my ride. Here's five to help out."

As Art put Ron's money into his pocket, he gave me a quick grin. I smiled back. Art may not have been too handsome, but he was fun to be with and he sure knew where it was at. Five dollars wasn't much, but it was twice as much as we'd had before. I was really beginning to have faith in Art. I knew he'd get us there somehow.

About an hour later I spotted a boy and girl. Art picked them up and before they got into the back he told them the same story he'd told Ron. I noticed a little smile on Ron's face. It was obvious he was on to Art's little game, but he seemed more amused by it than angry. Again Art showed the five dollars in his wallet; he didn't mention the five Ron had given him. The boy and girl each handed over two dollars and climbed into the back.

We stopped for gas in a short while and the bill came to nine dollars. Well, I thought, we still have our original five dollars, and I smiled contentedly.

The boy and girl left us and right after we crossed the Ohio line, we picked up a couple of boys. Art went through his act again, and this time each of them shelled out five dollars.

Ron left us, and as we drove on, we continued to pick up one or two hitchhikers to tide us over. Four days later, we arrived on the outskirts of San Francisco. Art pulled over to the side of the road and reached into his wallet—there was the five-dollar bill. Then he reached into his pocket and pulled out a bunch of crumpled bills.

We sat there and counted it out—just a little under fifty dollars. "This sure beats Bonnie and Clyde," I said, and we both laughed.

Art drove down to the Haight-Ashbury section. It was a big disappointment to me—it didn't look anything like

what I had thought it would, or like any of the pictures
I'd seen.

"Don't worry," Art. said. "I know a place that'll give
us some information on a free place to sleep."

We drove a few blocks, parked, and went into a small
office. I was a little shocked at Art, for as soon as I saw
the people running the place, I knew they were homosexu-
als. They ignored the fact that neither Art nor I was gay,
however, and went out of their way to be kind. They wrote
out an address where they said we could stay, and we
thanked them and returned to the van.

Art handed me the slip of paper. TWINKIES—STRANGE
THINGS AND ANTIQUE SHOP, 406 Burden Street, I read.

"How can we sleep in an antique shop ?" I asked.

"I don't know," Art said. "But that's what they gave us,
and I intend to find out."

We drove a few blocks more and I saw the two-story,
bright yellow building with a red-lettered sign: TWINKIES.
We parked and started into the shop, but I stopped stock-
still, halfway in and halfway out. I couldn't believe my
eyes! All kinds of strange things were hanging from the
ceiling. Straight ahead was a huge scaffold with a hang-
man's rope around it, and hanging from the rope was a
human skeleton. Hanging just beyond was a stuffed cow
with its two front legs missing, and its tongue hanging out.
Strung like Christmas decorations, from one side of the
room to the other, were books tied together with strips of
cloth. On the floor, right in front of me, was a bathroom
plunger. Right near it stood a full suit of armor.

I turned to flee back out again and on the wall above
the door I saw about twenty toilet seats, festooned with
long strands of toilet paper. Art pushed me in and closed
the door behind us. He took my hand, and we inched

forward a bit. No one seemed to be around; there wasn't a sound.

Suddenly, a siren went off. I jumped about a foot in the air and turned toward the door but, before I could go farther, a voice said, "Stop." I froze where I was; I was too scared to do anything else.

A loud, shrill laugh filled the room, and I turned my head slowly. There stood a man about five feet tall, dressed in a pink bloomer outfit. He had a long, white beard and wore a wide-brimmed hat. Elfin shoes with turned-up toes and a lion's tail completed his outfit.

I felt as though I were tripping on acid—everything was just too unreal. Then Art let out a whoop of laughter, and a little sanity returned. Could this be another gag of his? I wondered. Then I realized it was all as strange to him as it was to me, and I reached out and clung to his hand.

"Welcome home, my little children," the little old man said. "My friends at Freedom Home told me you were coming. I'm delighted to have you here. What are your names?"

"Becky Swenson."

"Art Koons." I noticed even voluble Art didn't offer any extra conversation.

The little man walked up to me and hugged me. I didn't know what to do, so I hugged him back. He embraced Art, too. Art just stood with his arms at his sides and submitted.

"Now, my children, you are invited to enjoy life here with me," the little old man said. "This is my palace of stars and what you see surrounding you is my great discovery of life.

"And now I want you to meet my chief assistant, Ring-A-Ding-Ding," he added.

He walked to the left side of the room and pulled a long rope that was hanging from the ceiling. There was a shrill whistle, and a girl of about eighteen appeared from behind a curtain. She smiled and reached out for my hand.

"Ring-A-Ding-Ding will show you to your rooms," the little old man said. "She'll tell you the rules when you get there."

The girl led us through the curtain, up some stairs, and into a very large room. There were about twenty cots in the room, and in one corner about five girls were sitting on the edge of a cot. Ring-A-Ding-Ding introduced us to the girls, then led Art out again.

I started to panic, but the girls reassured me. Next door was another big room, they said, and it was a boys' dormitory. We all ate together in a common kitchen, they said, but sleeping quarters were segregated by sex.

I asked the girls about the peculiar old man. None of them understood him or could figure him out. Several of the girls had been staying there for some time; a few had jobs; others had just come in a day or two before. No one was enthusiastic about the place, but they agreed that it was a roof over their heads.

One of the girls handed me a copy of the rules. I scanned them quickly. Number one was that all of our possessions had to be locked up in the old man's room; the second was that we all had to be locked in at night; the third was that we must remove our shoes before entering the kitchen; and the fourth, and last, forbade the use of toothbrushes—because of germs in the sink.

Even though I was dead tired, I slept fitfully that night. I woke at the slightest noise, and spent most of the night wishing Art were there. I could hardly wait for morning to come.

I saw Art at breakfast and I never was so glad to see anybody in my life! We both waited for a few others to enter the kitchen first, and sure enough everyone left his shoes outside the door. The kitchen itself made me think of an operating room—everything was white: the walls, the floor, the ceiling, the stove, the refrigerator. The whole room was immaculate. There wasn't a speck of dirt anywhere.

The breakfast was good, but I was so afraid I'd spill a crumb I didn't enjoy it much. Art and I decided we'd better clear out as soon as we finished eating, so we got Ring-A-Ding-Ding to get our things from the old man and took off.

I was despondent. Here we were in San Francisco, but where was the glamour, the fun? We had had plenty of excitement, but not the pleasurable kind.

As usual, Art was cheerful. He had the answers. We stopped at a phone booth and he riffled through the Yellow Pages until he came to the heading RUNAWAYS. He dialed the number, wrote down an address, and off we drove again.

This time the address was in a lovely residential area, and I relaxed. The house itself was a huge, old-style, three-story home, nestled among some trees.

A very attractive, middle-aged woman opened the door and invited us in. Art told her about his telephone call.

"Of course," she said, "we are happy to have you. Won't you come in?"

She led us into a big, comfortably furnished, sunny room.

"Do sit down," said this charming lady, "and I'll get you some coffee."

Art and I sat down on the sofa and smiled at each other.

We had lucked out; this was a lovely place that seemed too good to be true.

The charming lady returned and we all made small talk for a few minutes until coffee was brought in. The coffee was served by the weirdest-looking individual I'd ever seen—including the little old man in the bloomers! He was a very tall boy with absolutely no hair, and big circles had been painted around his eyes, like a clown in a circus.

At first I thought it was some kind of joke, but in a few moments two other boys came in and joined us for coffee. Both of them looked exactly like the first—no hair and black circles around their eyes. They all wore sweat shirts, jeans, and sandals.

The woman kept chatting away as though nothing unusual were going on, and I was hard put to think of anything to say. I was curious as all get-out, but I was afraid to ask about the boys. Art behaved as though everything were normal.

After we finished our coffee, our hostess excused herself for a minute, and I grabbed Art and headed out of the door. We didn't even stop to say thank you for the coffee.

We didn't say a word until we were cruising around in the van. Then I spoke up, almost in a wail, "I just can't believe any of this. Is all of San Francisco this way?"

Art laughed, as usual. "No, we just happened into two squirrelly places. Don't worry, I'll find us a decent place to stay."

We headed back toward Haight-Ashbury and Art decided we should walk around a little. We parked and it was nice to stroll around, but I kept worrying about where we'd stay. Pretty soon, Art struck up a conversation with a young couple.

It turned out they were runaways, and they said we

could stay at a pad they knew of. We went to the address they gave us, but I wasn't too hopeful; I was sure we'd run into more freaks.

Luck was with us this time, though. It wasn't much, but it was a place to sleep—one big room on the second floor of a building. The floor was covered with mattresses, and everyone just slept where he could find an empty spot. A lot of pot and hard drugs was floating around, but it certainly was a lot better than the two circuses we had just come from, and I was grateful to be around my own kind.

One morning a week later, I woke up and Art was not beside me. I looked around the room and my heart began to sink—no Art. I asked around and one girl said she had seen Art tiptoe out at dawn.

All that day, I walked the streets looking for him. All that night I hoped each newcomer was Art, but he never showed up. I spent a week hunting, and finally I had to admit he wasn't coming back. I didn't seem to have much luck with men—first Danny, now Art.

What was I to do? San Francisco wasn't all it was cracked up to be, that was for sure. And with no Art to look out for me, how was I going to manage? Without Art, I couldn't laugh at the crazy people, the dirty pads, the uncertainties—they scared me.

I had to admit that being on my own wasn't so hot. I longed for my own clean bed, the privacy of my own room. Home might not be much, but it was certainly better than this. I counted my money carefully. I had about $12.50 left from the money Art had given me.

It would have to do. I knew I was going to hitch back home.

3

When the girls at the pad learned I was taking off for the East, they gave me a lot of advice and a little money. One even gave me a small backpack she said would keep the cop off my back—they'd think I was a regular hiker.

Most of the advice was about rape, the greatest fear of all girl hitchhikers. Each one seemed to have a different tactic for averting rape. One said, "Tell him you have syphilis; he'll be scared to take the chance."

Another girl said, "Tell him you're underage; he won't dare risk it." The most approved method was to open the car door as if to jump out—especially if another car was following closely. This would supposedly scare the guy so he'd pull over and let you out! (It scared me, too! I couldn't imagine jumping out of a speeding car.)

All of them warned me that if any or all of these tactics failed, I was to submit quietly and not fight back or I would face almost certain death. They all laid down one other rule: If you have a gut feeling that something is wrong, turn the ride down, even if you have to jump out after the car starts.

I was grateful for the advice. I realized that my one ride out with Art didn't qualify me as an experienced hitch-hiker. I had been awfully lucky. But I was anxious to get going, and I was confident I could look after myself.

Hours later, trudging down the highway, I wasn't so

confident. It was almost noon and I had gotten only one short ride.

I was on the outskirts of Hankin when a dumpy, old black pickup pulled up to the curb just a little ahead of me. I started to run up, then hesitated as I saw an old, barefoot guy get out. I watched as he sat on the curb and tried to put his shoes on.

"How come you're getting out?" I asked him. Somehow, I had a funny feeling about the old guy. But he ignored me and kept fumbling with his shoes; he acted drunk.

A voice called from the truck, "Want a ride, kid?"

Gut feeling or no, I needed a ride. As I got closer to the truck I decided they didn't look too bad, after all. The old guy needed a shave, but the young one was quite nice looking.

The young fellow jumped out, helped me into the truck, and climbed in after me. "Hi, I'm Ned," he said, "and this is Hank."

"I'm Becky," I replied. "Are you father and son?"

"Yes," said Hank. "He's the father and I'm his son."

I laughed politely as Hank reached over and shifted gears, and we started off. As he returned the gear to the drive position, he slipped his hand onto my knee. I looked over at him, but he was staring at the highway.

I pushed his hand over; he put it back, and I pushed it away again. When he put it back a third time, his fingers dug in hard; I left the hand where it was—the gut feeling was returning. I was going to have to figure out how to handle these guys.

Ned reached into his pocket and said, "Here's something for you."

I watched fearfully, praying he wasn't going to pull out

a gun or a switchblade. He handed me a joint and I breathed a sigh of relief. I thanked him and all three of us lit up. I was feeling pretty good when Ned offered me some downers. I popped a few, and soon my fears disappeared. Everything looked rosy and I was getting drowsy.

"How about taking a shortcut to Salisbury? We can save a little time," Hank asked Ned.

"Fine. Okay with you?" Ned asked me.

"Anything to speed the trip up," I replied as we turned off onto an asphalt road. Soon we turned left onto a gravel road and then into another that was just two ruts.

"Hank, let's show this girl our marijuana field," Ned said.

"That's a good idea. It's been a while since we checked the leaves; some of them ought to be about ready to pick."

"Do you guys really grow your own marijuana?" I asked incredulously.

Hank laughed. "Now you know I'm not about to admit that to anybody. But, if you're a good little girl, we might let you take a quick look—even pick a leaf or two—if you won't tell anyone."

I was still drifting along on the pills, so I said, "I pledge on my honor I won't breathe a word."

The ruts ended and we all piled out of the truck. I looked around expectantly, but Hank dropped to the ground and said, "We'll wait here until we're sure we're not being followed."

Ned sat down nearby and pulled me down next to him. He put his arm around my shoulder. "Nothing doing," I said, and pushed him away.

He laughed and pushed me to the ground. I slapped him and, in desperation, kicked him in the groin. He let out a howl and rolled over on his side.

"That'll teach you," I said, and scrambled to get up. But Ned grabbed my hair and jerked me back. As I raised my hand to slap him again, he flicked a switchblade out of his pocket with his other hand and jammed it against my throat.

"Listen, Becky," he said, "no yelling, no screaming, no nothing. Get that?"

I got it. I could taste the fear in my mouth. Reluctantly, I dropped my hand to my side and submitted quietly— first to Ned, then to Hank. Mercifully, it was over quickly. I lay where they had left me, my mind blank, dry sobs racking my body.

Ned shoved the switchblade back into his pocket, then walked over and stared down at me. "I'm sorry," he stammered. "I really didn't mean to do it. You got me mad."

I turned my back; I was afraid I was going to throw up.

"Okay, back to the truck," Hank said.

Ned reached down and helped me up and over to the truck. I managed to push him into the middle and then pulled myself up next to him. No one said a word on the long trip back to the highway. Hank stopped to let me out, but Ned insisted he drive me on to the outskirts of the next town.

As I jumped out of the truck, Ned threw some change after me. I scrambled around the edge of the highway picking it up, as they drove off. A phone booth was just up ahead and I needed that change. I knew I could never hitch all the way back after this experience. All I could think of to do was call my folks and ask if they'd send me carfare home.

As I listened to the phone ring and ring, I prayed they'd take me back. I could never tell them about the rape—I could never tell anyone; I felt dirty all over—but I badly needed a safe haven and home was all I could think of.

When my mother finally answered, she was so glad to hear me she didn't ask any questions. She said for me to get to the nearest airport and she'd see that a ticket was there for me.

"And Becky," she closed, "we have a big surprise for you. We've been so hoping you'd call."

"I'll be there waiting for the ticket," I told her. "I'll see you soon."

I walked on up the road to a diner and ordered some coffee. While the waitress was getting it, I went into the ladies' room, ripped out the seams of my bra, and took out the ten dollars I had sewed in before I left San Francisco.

Luckily for me, the airport was nearby, and a bus going there stopped at the diner regularly. I was there in about half an hour. I whiled away the time there, wondering what surprise my parents could have for me. My mind seemed to be functioning normally; my body was sore, but my mind seemed to have blanked out my recent experience.

It wasn't long before my name was called over the public-address system—my ticket was there. I picked it up and got on board a plane, still puzzling over the surprise. What could it be? Wheels of my own? That was too good to be true! The trip abroad my parents had been talking about for years? A horse, maybe—all my life I'd wanted a horse. At last, I dozed off and slept most of the long trip home.

The first person I saw was my mother, and she was crying. I didn't know whether to laugh or cry, so I just ran up to her and threw my arms around her. She hugged me back so hard I thought my ribs might crack, but that hug was a big relief. It told me I was accepted and everything was going to be all right.

There were a million things I wanted to say to Mom, but the words just wouldn't come out. I wanted to tell her I was sorry for making her worry and how glad I was to be back. Fortunately, Mom chattered on about nothing most of the way home, until I finally got the words out.

"Mom, I'm sorry I ran away," I said. "Do you forgive me?"

The tears welled up in her eyes again and she said, "Becky, you don't know what these hours and days and weeks of not hearing from you have done to me. I've lain awake nights worrying about you. I thought about kidnapping. I thought about rape. I pictured you in jail. Now, thank God, you're home."

I choked up and couldn't say anything. Here I'd been cursing out my mother while I'd been away, and she'd been worrying about me the whole time. I felt like a heel. Suddenly I remembered the surprise she had mentioned on the phone.

"Say, what's this great big surprise you've got for me?" I asked.

"It's too involved to explain while I'm driving down the highway," she said. "I'll tell you all about it when we get home, and that won't be long at the rate we're going. Not much traffic today."

"Can't you give me a hint?" I asked.

"No, I can't," she said testily. "I told you it's a long story. All I'll say is it's something your father and I have discussed for a long time."

I bit my tongue on more questions; I didn't want to make her madder. From the sound of it, it must be the trip to Europe, and at the moment I wanted more travel like I wanted a hole in my head.

It wasn't long before we pulled into our driveway. I hopped out of the car and dashed into the house—it all looked so good and familiar. "I'm going to take a shower," I yelled at Mom, "and then I've got to hear about the surprise."

It was wonderful to get a hot shower and step into clean clothes. I enjoyed every minute of it. Then I returned to the living room, pulled Mom gently down on the sofa, and said, "Come on, out with it. What's the surprise? Is it a horse? You know how I've always wanted one. Dad said we could board it at that stable down the road? Is that it? Or a car of my own?"

"No, it's none of those things," Mom said. "I told you it's a long story."

"Well, get on with it," I said impatiently. "What can be better than wheels of my own?"

"Becky, Becky, calm down," my mother said. "You'll have to let me tell it my own way.

"Shortly after you ran away," she began, "Mrs. Stager called me and asked if I would serve on the advisory committee of the new Mental Health Center. I told her I knew nothing about mental health and I was too upset worrying about you to do anything. She insisted that it would be good for me and that I could help other girls, so in the end she talked me into doing it."

"Get to the point, will you?" I snapped. "What has any of this to do with me or a surprise?"

"Well, to make a long story short, I've talked the head psychiatrist at the center into taking your case."

"Taking my case?" I screamed. "Since when am I a case? Now that you're a big advisory member I'm no longer your daughter, I'm just a number, a case for your doctor friends to practice on!"

"You don't know Dr. Armour—he's the head of the clinic and a wonderful man. He's so kind and understanding, I just *know* he will help you with all your problems and you'll be the sunny, happy girl we used to know."

I was so mad I almost burst. No good-for-nothing shrink was going to try out all his theories on me, I was determined. Too many kids I met in San Francisco, and even before I left home, had been through psychoanalysis and I didn't know one who had been helped. A lot had run away from home just to get away from the psychiatrists!

The more Mother explained all the doctor had to offer, the more determined I became. But I knew if I kept on arguing we'd only wind up in one big fight, so I just said, "We'll talk about it later," and headed back to my room.

Just then, my father came in the front door. I hesitated a moment, then said, "Hi, Dad, I'm back."

"Hello, Becky," Dad replied, and walked on into the living room.

I went in my room and closed the door behind me. I had so hoped from Mom's telephone conversation that things had changed around here, but home was no different: Mom still had crazy ideas and Dad his bad moods.

I thought of Nora, a girl I had met in San Francisco. She had run away from a really wealthy family in Alabama. When I asked her if she wouldn't rather go back home instead of begging for food and sleeping on filthy mattresses, she said, "Never. Home is hell."

Well, this might not be hell, but it certainly wasn't the heaven I'd been imagining all the way back. A home is a lot more than just four walls, or money, or a car, but at the moment, I couldn't figure out exactly what it took to make one.

4

For the next few days, I stayed close to my room. I was sleeping poorly, having nightmares about Ned and Hank. I swiped a few of Mom's sleeping pills, but they didn't help much. My conscious mind still seemed to have blanked out the rape, but I thought more about the abortion and the daily fights we all had when I did venture out of my room. I became more and more depressed.

One night, when I woke from a nightmare, drenched with sweat, I knew I had had enough. I grabbed a blanket, went to the bathroom and got Mom's pills, and crept on into the kitchen. I stuffed the blanket carefully around the bottom of the closed door, filled a glass with water and downed as many of the barbiturates as I could swallow, and turned on all the gas jets. Then I sat down to wait.

The next thing I knew someone was slapping my face hard. "Wake up, wake up, Becky," my mother's voice came through a fog. She continued to slap me, but somehow I couldn't pry my eyes open or answer her.

"What's the matter with you? Haven't you any sense at all?" she asked as she continued to slap and shake me. "I've got to get you to a hospital. How many pills did you take?"

"I didn't count," I managed to mumble. My eyes started to focus and I saw my father burst into the room.

"What happened?" he yelled.

"I don't know," my mother said. "I couldn't sleep and

I thought I heard something in the kitchen, so I came out to investigate. I smelled gas, but couldn't get the door open at first. Finally, I pushed it open and there was Becky lying on the floor, with this empty bottle of pills next to her. I turned off the gas jets and opened the window."

My father reached down, grabbed my bathrobe, and lifted me to my feet. His face, beet-red, was right in mine.

"What are you trying to do?" he roared. "Is this the way you repay your mother and father for what they've done for you? Well, I'll tell *you* something. Attempted suicide is against the law. You can go to jail for something like this—understand that?"

My head wobbled and my knees gave way; only Dad's tight grip held me up.

"I'm going to call an ambulance," my mother said. "She looks as though she's dying right now." She ran from the room.

I kept my eyes closed. I was disgusted that I had failed at suicide, but I was rather enjoying all the attention.

Mother came rushing back into the kitchen, where Dad had propped me up in a chair. "If I call an ambulance and the attendants know she's tried to commit suicide, will they call the cops?" she asked my father. "They're liable to ask a lot of questions and we can all wind up in serious trouble."

"I don't know," he answered. "The best thing to do is just ask them to pump out her stomach—just say something she ate made her sick and then she passed out."

"You'd better be right," Mother said. "It seems to me Becky's nothing but trouble—first an abortion, now a suicide attempt. Next thing we know we might have a murder on our hands."

I opened my eyes. "Thanks, Mother," I said sarcastically. "All you seem to do is worry about your own image. If I pull out of this, maybe I *will* knock somebody off, just so you can see me fry in the electric chair!"

My father grabbed me again. "Stop that right now," he said, and began to drag me down the hall.

I fought back with what little strength I had, but it didn't do any good. I wound up in the bathroom with my head over the toilet bowl. Dad grabbed two of my fingers and pushed them into my mouth.

"Vomit up those pills, right now," he ordered.

I tried to talk and to pull my hand out, but he jammed the fingers clear down my throat. "Puke," he said, "puke."

I started to retch, but nothing came up as he forced the fingers mercilessly down and down until I thought I would choke. Finally, it took effect—I vomited and vomited, and seemed unable to stop.

At long last, Dad loosened his grip and pulled me up. "Why'd you do it, Becky?" he asked.

I looked at him groggily, but didn't answer. He propped me up while Mother sponged me off. Then he carried me back to my bed and laid me down gently. The two of them stood there and looked down at me.

"I won't do that again," I told them.

"I hope not. You scared us to death," my mother said. Then the two of them went to their room. I heard their voices for a few minutes, then Mom returned and sat on the edge of my bed. She didn't say anything, but once she passed her hand over my tangled hair. In a moment, I drifted off to sleep.

When I awoke, she was gone. I glanced over at the clock —it hardly seemed possible that little more than an hour had passed since I had crept out to the kitchen. I lifted my head carefully. I was still groggy, but my mind was clear enough to be disgusted at my suicide failure. Nothing had changed, and I was determined to end it all—right now, if I could.

I staggered to the bathroom, balancing myself against the wall, and listening for any sound. Everything was quiet. It seemed hours before I reached the safety of the bathroom and this time I closed the door slowly and quietly before I locked it: I wasn't going to be interrupted again! I took my father's razor from the medicine cabinet, slid the blade out, and looked at it. It didn't look big enough to do the job; all I could do was hope it was sharp. I jabbed at my wrist, but only a few ineffectual nicks appeared. I gritted my teeth, steadied myself against the bowl, and slashed at the wrist again, this time more forcefully.

At last some blood appeared, but only a trickle or two. I thought I heard a noise and I slashed frantically again and again. This time I succeeded; the blood spurted out. I cut like a madwoman, until the bowl was running red and I was feeling dizzy. Vague voices sounded in my ears, as my head spun and my hand rose and fell, wielding the razor blade. I could feel myself falling, and then I knew no more.

"The cuts are pretty deep," I heard a voice say, "but I think I have them stanched now. She really should be in a hospital, but I know the gossip mongers in this town and I hate to put you all through that. I'll sew them up here, and look at them again tomorrow, to be sure."

Dimly I recognized the voice of our family doctor. "Dr. Jensen, how did you get here?" I asked.

"How do you suppose?" he asked severely. "Your father called me after that first silly attempt of yours. He wanted to be sure all of the poison was out of your system. And a good thing he did, too. I got here just as you started this one and he was tearing the bathroom door off its hinges."

"I hated to bother you at this time of night," my father started, but the doctor cut him off. "After all the years we've known each other? Don't be ridiculous; that's what I'm here for, in case of emergency."

He gave a little laugh, and added, "Although I hope you don't have many like this one. Now you two clear out and Becky and I will get on with what has to be done."

My parents hesitated, looked at each other, and left the room reluctantly. "Can't I help?" my father asked.

"Just put the door back up after we finish," the doctor said, and turned to me in a businesslike manner. "It's not going to be any picnic, Becky, it'll hurt a lot, so just hang on and grit your teeth. Don't you dare pass out on me again. I'll give you a shot, but it won't kill all the pain."

He gave me the shot, washed up the wounds as gently as he could, and proceeded to sew them up. He was right; the pain was excruciating, but I looked the other way, gritted my teeth, and hung on.

Finally he finished, lifted me in his arms, and carried me to my bedroom, where he dumped me unceremoniously on the bed. He flopped into the nearby chair and gave a huge sigh. I never saw a wearier-looking man in my life.

"Well, we did it, Becky," he said. "You're going to be all right. You'll be sore for a while; I'll have to dress those wounds a few times, but you're going to be okay.

"I'll give you a sedative to make you sleep, before I go," he added. "But, tell me one thing, Becky—why did you do it? Why the gas? the pills? the razor? You're only a kid.

I've known you since you were a baby. Seems to me you've got a lot to look forward to."

"What?" I blurted out, and then the tears began. "I don't want to talk about it," I sobbed.

Doctor Jensen got up and sat down on the edge of my bed and started to stroke my hair. "There, there, Becky, cry; it'll do you good. Tell me what's bothering you. Get it out of your system."

I cried harder. "You'll tell—my parents and everyone else. I'll never be able to face anyone again. I've got nothing to live for."

"Stop that, Becky," the doctor snapped. "Stop feeling sorry for yourself. That's what most of the trouble is. Come on, talk, let it all out. I promise you, on my word of honor, I'll never tell a soul what you tell me here."

What did I have to lose? I blurted it all out: the problems with Danny—how he had promised to marry me until the abortion—how Art left me; about the pastor and my guilt feelings; even about Ned and Hank. It all poured out in a jumble.

Doctor Jensen listened without saying a word; he hardly moved a muscle except to stroke my hair occasionally.

When I finally finished, we both just sat there, staring at each other. "Doctor," I asked, "do you believe in life after death?"

"Why do you ask?"

"Oh, I just wondered. I've heard that most doctors don't. Tell me, honestly: Do you believe there is life after death?"

He straightened up and stared across the room for a moment. "No, I don't," he said slowly. "Do you?"

"I don't know," I answered.

"Well, why did you ask me that question?"

"I didn't succeed in committing suicide tonight. One of these days maybe I will. But if you don't believe in life after death, why didn't you let me die?"

I waited for his answer. It was a long time in coming and it sounded as though he were thinking it out as he said it. "I see what you're driving at. You want me to say that suicide is okay, that it's *your* life. If a person wants to commit suicide it's for him to decide, because it's *his* life and no one else's.

"I'm against suicide because of the grief it causes people —those who are left behind. Those people are always saying, 'If only I'd. . . . ' " His voice trailed off.

"Believe me, Becky," he started again, "I've seen men commit suicide and their families have mourned for years. The guy is dead, but what about his family? You may succeed at suicide, but what about your mother and father?"

I could see it now—Mom and Dad standing over my casket, weeping. I wanted to hurt them and this would hurt them badly—or would it? Might they be relieved? Hadn't Mom cited the trouble I caused?

"I'm going to get you that sedative I promised," the doctor said. He returned in a moment and handed me a glass of water and a pill. I swallowed obediently.

"It's been a long night, Becky," he said. "I'll let myself out. Rest assured I'll never breathe a word to a living soul, but you remember and think about what I said. Your parents love you and they're doing the best they can. Life has a lot to offer you. Cheer up." He leaned over, brushed his lips across my forehead, and walked out.

As I waited for the pill to take effect, my thoughts raced. They were all jumbled up: I wanted to get even with my parents, but was the doctor right? Would my father have torn the door off its hinges if he hadn't cared? Would they even have called the doctor if they hadn't cared?

Here I was—sixteen years old—and I had already had more happen to me than most women of forty. Could it be my fault? Was the doctor right about life after death? The thoughts became fuzzier and fuzzier. Sleep came.

5

The next morning, I awoke early and thought about my conversation with the doctor the night before. I decided that although my parents really made life rough for me at times, I really didn't hate them. Did they love me? One sure way to find out was to ask.

I heard my parents moving around in the kitchen and got up to have breakfast with them—something I rarely did. When I walked into the kitchen, fully clothed, my father almost fell out of his chair.

"What in the world are you doing up so early?" he asked.

"Oh, I just thought I'd have breakfast with you. It kind of feels good to be alive this morning," I said.

"That's not funny, Becky," my mother snapped.

"Now, Sylvia, don't get so uptight," Dad admonished her.

"It's too early in the morning. Besides, *I'm* happy that Becky is alive this morning. So are you. She didn't mean it the way it sounded."

I tried to make conversation, but Mom and Dad ate their eggs and toast in complete silence. I wondered if they always ate their breakfast without exchanging a word with each other. I realized they were both still upset over last night, and I was sorry I'd caused them so much trouble, but I *had* to find out if they loved me.

"Mom, I want to ask you a flat-out question: Do you love me?"

Mom dropped her fork and just stared at me. She didn't say a word.

I turned toward Dad. "Do you love me?"

He looked at Mom helplessly, then down at his plate. "Why, of course we love you," Mom rallied. "What makes you think we don't? That's a silly question to ask. You're our daughter, aren't you? Now tell me, why did you ask that question?"

"Because I really wanted to know," I told them.

Dad shoved his chair back and walked quickly into the living room. I stared after him.

"Mom, do you think Dad really loves me?" I asked.

"Of course he loves you, honey. Oh, I know he can be short-tempered, but when has he really given you reason to think he doesn't love you?"

"Oh, I don't know," I mumbled. It was hard to explain, but I tried. "Why do fathers take love for granted? Why doesn't he ever tell me he loves me? Most of all, why doesn't he ever hug me or do *something* so I can feel his love without his having to tell me?"

"I know I've caused you both a lot of trouble. Do you think you'd be happier in this household if I'd never been born?"

"Don't be silly," my mother snapped. "Of course not. But I will be honest, Becky. You *have* caused us a lot of grief. You have hurt me badly and at times I have thought the hurt your Dad felt might destroy him. After all, we are both human and there is just so much we can take.

"He's been very upset over your behavior lately, and it's made him more irritable than usual. He has lost his temper so much at work that they've threatened to fire him if he doesn't shape up. That's not like him, and that ultimatum has upset him still more. He's afraid of losing his job, and he's worried sick over what you may do next."

I stared at my mother in amazement. It looked as if the doctor was right—maybe my parents did care. I had never thought that the way I acted affected my dad one way or the other, and I was always trying to get a rise out of him. Could *I* be the one who was destroying our home, not the other way around?

I got up and walked into the living room, where Dad was sitting on the sofa, staring at his feet. For the first time in my life I felt sorry for him. I had never really looked at him before; I just took him for granted, like a piece of furniture. He looked tired and unhappy.

"Becky, come here and sit down by me," he said. "I don't really know what to say—or do—about your running away and your suicide attempts. I suppose I have failed you as a father somehow. But it isn't too late. Something's wrong and we've got to find the answer."

I knew I had to find some way to help my dad. "What do you want me to do?" I asked.

Two big tears started to trickle down his cheek and he reached into his back pocket, pulled out a handkerchief and blew his nose hard, and swiped at his face.

"There is something that might possibly help you," he said slowly.

"What is it? I'll do it," I said quickly. I wanted to do anything, no matter how difficult, to get that sad look off my dad's face.

"I suppose your mother has told you about her work at the Mental Health Center? Well, I have gotten to know Dr. Armour, and he has taken an interest in you. He says he can really help you, and I believe him."

I couldn't believe my ears! No wonder he had such a

rough life, with my mother and her nutty ideas. Here she had sold him a bill of goods on this psychiatry kick of hers. Gone were my thoughts of helping my dad: I felt only rage.

"Dont give me any of that Dr. Armour garbage. That dirty mother of mine tricked me into coming home by making big promises! If you think that shrink can help me, you're sadly mistaken. I will never, never, never go to him!" I screamed.

Dad looked at me hopelessly as I continued to rant and rave. I finally ran out of steam and he said to me, quietly, "Becky, will you do me just one favor—just this once? Will you *please*, and I say please with all the sincerity I can muster, just spend two minutes with Dr. Armour?"

I started to scream again, but stopped immediately. Dad's voice was so shaky and he looked so forlorn, I just couldn't carry on anymore.

"All right," I agreed grudgingly. "I'll go just once—for you. I dont want Mom to think she's got me convinced."

"Any way you want," Dad said hastily. "I'll call Dr. Armour right away and see when we can get an appointment, and I won't say a word to your mother."

The next evening when we left for the appointment with Dr. Armour, my mother wanted to go along. "Oh, we're just going down town for a milk shake," Dad said hurriedly. "Can't a man spend a little time with a pretty girl who isn't his wife?" he added jokingly. Mom smiled, and I could guess what she was thinking—at last my dad was going to spend more time with me and act like a father.

"Okay, have a good time," she said, and closed the door behind us.

Doctor Armour had no receptionist, so we sat in the

empty waiting room alone. In a few minutes a door off the reception room opened, and a young man in a white jacket walked in.

"Good evening, Mr. Swenson," he said. "Sorry if I've kept you waiting." He turned to me and stuck out his hand. "And you must be Becky."

"How do you do, Dr. Armour," I replied politely. My mind was racing. All my preconceived notions were wrong so far. I had thought all headshrinkers were baldish, older men with oily voices. This guy was young, good-looking, and built like a football player!

He grasped my hand with both of his and drew me to my feet. "Becky," he said, "come on into the office with me for a few minutes so we can talk comfortably. Excuse us, Mr. Swenson."

I glanced around the office—sure enough, there was the famous psychiatrist's couch. But he didn't ask me to get on it; he led me gently to a big, overstuffed chair and waved me into it.

His appearance and his actions unnerved me. They were so unlike my friends' tales of visits to psychiatrists. I was still suspicious, because everyone I knew who had seen a shrink told me about ending up with more problems than he or she had before. I wondered what approach he would use.

"Do you hate your mother?" he asked.

"Yes."

"Your father?"

"Yes. . . . Well, I did, but now I'm not so sure. I, well, I. . . . " I didn't know how to answer.

Then he asked, "Do you hate yourself?"

That floored me. Hate myself? There were times I wasn't too proud of myself or of things I'd done, and I was trying to find some answers to life that I couldn't seem to find, but hate myself? That was a new idea.

"No, I don't think so," I finally said.

"Now, Becky, I want you to sit on the edge of the couch and do a few simple exercises for me," he said. "Put your arms straight out to the side," he instructed, after I climbed onto the couch.

I did as I was told.

"Now tell me what you feel," Dr. Armour said.

"This is stupid," I said, and let my arms drop. "I don't feel anything, except that my arms are getting tired."

"All right, we'll skip the exercises," the doctor said, and he walked over and stood directly in front of me.

"Do you mind if I touch you?" he asked.

I looked at him suspiciously. Was he going to get fresh?

"Where?" I asked.

"Oh, anyplace," he replied.

"Anyplace?" Well, I decided, my own father brought me here and he says trust this guy, so here goes.

"Okay," I said.

I held my breath while Dr. Armour reached out to me slowly. He rubbed his hand gently against my cheek and asked again. "What do you feel?"

"Your hand on my cheek. What am I supposed to feel?"

"Do you feel love?"

"No, I feel the sweat of your hand."

Doctor Armour pulled his hand back quickly and returned to his seat behind his desk.

"What did you want me to do, when I rubbed your cheek?" he asked.

I decided to be honest. "I wanted you to lean down and kiss me."

"Well, that isn't a bad idea; you're an attractive young

lady." He smiled. "Do you know what your answer—the first honest one you've given me—tells me?"

"What?"

"That you are a girl who needs a lot of affection and is craving love," he said. "That's all for tonight, but you come see me every week for a few weeks and I'm going to show you how to get some real love in your life, so you won't have to run away or do desperate things to get it."

For the next six weeks or so I went to Dr. Armour faithfully each week. I really didn't get anything out of the sessions, but Dad seemed pathetically pleased that I continued to go.

At first the doctor went back to having me do exercises and describe my feelings. I really didn't feel anything at all, so I made up stuff by the yard and told it to him with a straight face.

Later, he started to probe my sex life, and he asked me to describe it in detail. I had the time of my life making up wild tales. I told about relations with businessmen and lawyers, and I described in detail how a doctor had seduced me during a physical exam. I didn't see how he could swallow it all, but he seemed to accept it as truth.

After one session, I asked Dr. Armour a few questions. He was very free with his answers and seemed perfectly willing to talk. He had been married for four years, I learned, and had a little girl who lived with his wife after their divorce. I questioned him about his attitude toward drugs. Much to my surprise, he admitted that he smoked pot once in a while.

"Why, Dr. Armour," I said, "I'm shocked. Just a few weeks ago, you were telling me I should give up drugs, and now you say you take them!"

"I didn't say that," he protested. "I only smok

marijuana cigarette once in a blue moon, not regularly. To be honest, I think it should be legalized."

"What kind of feeling do you get when you smoke it?" I asked.

"A very soothing one," he replied. "Very relaxing."

"Doctor, put your arms out to your sides," I grinned at him. "Then tell me what you feel."

He started to do as I instructed and then we both broke up laughing at the reversal of our roles. That was the end of that session.

During the next week, I thought about our conversations. What a phony that guy was. He was supposed to be helping me, and he used marijuana as a crutch himself. It was just as I had thought —all shrinks are phonies. I was a little disappointed, as I had gotten so I liked him and rather enjoyed the visits. Then the thought hit me—if he's so lenient about marijuana, maybe he'll give me some uppers or downers. I decided to try him out on the next visit.

"Doctor Armour," I said, "you have really been helping me a lot, but I still feel in a constant state of turmoil. I'm sure if I could just calm down a bit, I could figure out a good value system of life. Isn't there something you could give me that would help?"

"No problem at all," he said promptly. "I'll give you a prescription for tranquilizers and they will calm you down so you can think things through."

That evening I went down to the drugstore and filled my prescription, then I went home and took a couple of pills. It didn't take long for me to feel high, and I was happy. I laughed to myself; here I was going to the doctor to keep my parents happy, and he was keeping me happy by keeping me high. It was crazy!

The next week, when I went to keep my appointment, a nurse was sitting at the reception desk. She took me into Dr. Armour's office and introduced me to a man sitting at Armour's desk.

"Doctor Whitmore, this is Becky Swenson," she said.

"But where is Dr. Armour?" I asked.

"He isn't in today," Dr. Whitmore replied, "but I'll be glad to talk to you."

I didn't like the looks of this new doctor. He made me think of my old picture of a psychiatrist: he was baldish, middle-aged, and ugly. I didn't like his manner, either. He seemed very cold, after Dr. Armour.

As soon as the nurse left, the doctor looked at me and said, "You've been playing games, haven't you? You know what I mean, you smart little brat. You've been taking advantage of Dr. Armour for a good, long while, and now you're into him for drugs. I've been over your file and I know your kind.

"Get this straight, kid. Do it my way, or you're never going to make it. You'll go crazy or die."

If this was shock treatment, I didn't like it. "Good," I said, "I hate living anyway."

"You listen to me, young lady; I was an alcoholic, but I stopped drinking—I'm completely cured. I'm going to help you stop this running away, the drug bit, and the depression, too, but it's going to be hard. Nothing that's worthwhile is easy."

I just glared at him. If he thought I was going to help him, he was crazy.

"I'm going to help you change your life, girl," he said urgently, and grabbed hold of my arm. "It's just a question of mind over matter. You change your thinking and *you* can change. It worked for me and it can work for you. I'll *make* it work for you."

"Get your filthy paws off me," I told him, jerked myself free, and stormed out of his office.

"What happened to Dr. Armour?" I asked the nurse again.

"Doctor Armour is no longer with us," she said primly. "I'm not permitted to reveal the details. He has changed his place of residency for a while. That's about all I can say. Doctor Whitmore is taking over his practice, for the time being."

"Well, I'm not going to be one of his patients," I told her, and slammed out of the office.

When I got home, my mother and father were sitting at the kitchen table having a cup of coffee.

"Dad," I burst out, "you can't imagine what happened at the doctor's office this afternoon! Doctor Armour wasn't there. A guy by the name of Whitmore was there instead and he started to rough me up."

I waited for Dad's indignation, but it didn't come. He looked down at his coffee and stirred it again.

"What happened to Dr. Armour?" I demanded.

"I meant to tell you before you left, but I didn't get a chance" Dad said finally. "His office called me and told me about Dr. Whitmore. Then, when I read this morning's paper, I saw a short piece that said Dr. Armour had been arrested for possession of and sale of marijuana."

I ran to my room and slammed the door. I didn't like the way Dad had told me, and it seemed funny that he hadn't told me before I left. What had Dr. Whitmore told him? I went to the closet and took my tranquilizers out of their hiding place.

I was mad at my father. I was mad at my mother, I was mad at Dr. Armour, and I was especially mad at Dr. Whitmore. Nuts to the whole bunch of them, I thought, and swallowed a few of the pills.

There was a knock on the door, followed immediately by my father bursting into the room. He was in a rage, madder, I think, than I had ever seen him. He took off his belt and came toward me.

"So Dr. Whitmore was right! That's why you don't like him; he's on to you. He told me you were getting drugs from Dr. Armour. All these months, we've been paying out a fortune to get you well, and you've been fooling us all the time. Well, no daughter of mine is going to become a drug addict!"

He grabbed the telltale bottle out of my hand and started to whale me with the belt. He continued to beat me until he was exhausted and I was halfway passed out; I didn't know whether it was from the pills or the beating, but I felt little pain.

At last he left and I fell into a doze. Full sleep would not come; the pain of the beating was beginning to come through. I tried to get up, but the pain was too much and I dropped back as I heard another knock at the door.

I cowered as the door opened. Was Dad going to start again? But this time it was my mother.

"Becky," she said, "we've got to talk."

"About what?" I asked. "I'm in no shape for more of your nutty ideas."

"About all of us," she said, "and this time you'll have to listen. I've tried before, but you've paid no attention."

"Can't it wait? I'm in no shape for a lecture. I'm in too much pain."

"No, it can't wait," she said flatly. "You're not the only

one in pain. We are all aching and bruised all over. Because of the problems we're having with you, your father and I have developed our own set of problems. Our marriage is no longer a happy one: we cannot agree on anything. If you don't straighten up, you'll be the cause of our divorce. You can see the shape you've gotten your father into.

"If it comes to divorce, you'll have to decide with whom you are going to live," she added.

I stared at her. I couldn't think of anything to say. Finally, she turned on her heel and walked out.

Her words shook me up. Divorce had never occurred to me. Through the pain, I couldn't think clearly. Mom was forever on my back; I certainly didn't want to live alone with her. Living alone with Dad would be taking my life in my hands.

At long last, I slept. When I awoke, I ached all over, but the sharp pain was gone. I thought about my mother's words and I could come up with only one answer: I would have to leave home again.

This time, it would probably be for good, for not only was I miserable myself but I was wrecking my parents' lives also. Maybe my departure would bring peace to the family.

6

I walked and walked—I don't know for how long—sticking out my thumb at each oncoming car, but no one stopped. I saw a yellow Cadillac in the distance, put on my brightest smile, waved my arm, and got almost in its path. It worked: the driver pulled up and threw the door open.

"Hop in," he said, "where are you going?"

I was still in a pretty somber mood, despite the glued-on smile, and I really hadn't thought up a story yet, so I blurted out the truth. "I have no idea where I'm going, so long as I'm going," I said.

"That sounds like a great idea. Like to try it myself sometime," the driver responded.

His voice was nice; I took a better look at him and decided I liked him.

"Unless you've got some important errands, why don't you join me heading toward I-don't-know-where?" I asked jokingly.

"I've got a better idea," he answered. "Why don't you come along with me?"

"I'm not that kind of girl," I quickly responded.

He started to laugh. "I know what kind of girl you are. I know you. You're Becky Swenson, aren't you?"

"How in the world do you know that?"

"You have a friend named Lenny Schwartz. Right?"

Lenny was a boy who lived down the block from me. He was nineteen, and I had gone out with him a few times before I met Danny. Lenny was a nice guy and he had connections, so he could get the best stuff—uppers, downers, heroin, acid, speed, marijuana.

"Yes, I'm a friend of Lenny's," I said carefully. "What's that got to do with it?"

"Well, I'm Lenny's cousin David, and we met at his place one night. You may not remember it, because you were high and I doubt you remember much about the whole night."

I didn't want to admit that I had ever gotten that high, so I said, "Why, of course, now I remember you, David."

"I guess that makes us properly introduced," David said, and laughed. "Since we've got the preliminaries all over with, why don't you tell me what you are really up to?"

I decided the best thing to do was level with him. "To tell you the truth, I'm running away from home. Things got so bad that I tried to commit suicide, but it didn't work. Now I had a big fight with my old man and my old lady, so I decided I'd better take off and see what the rest of the world is doing."

"Is that bandage on your arm the result of trying to do yourself in?"

"Yes."

"Well," he said slowly, "if you want to, you can come and stay with me. But don't you ever try to commit suicide at my place. So help me, if you ever try that, I'll take your body and throw it in the river. I don't believe in that sort of thing and I can't afford to have someone like you messing up my life. I've got a great thing going and no one is going to spoil it for me."

"Whatever it is you've got going, this beautiful Caddy is certainly getting you there," I said. "Just what is your game?"

"My father left me twelve big oil wells in Texas," he said shortly.

I laughed, but I realized I wasn't going to learn much from him on that score. I needed a place to stay badly and what better place than with a guy who owned a Cadillac? Maybe I could live like the rich!

"I promise, David, that I will not try to commit suicide so long as I am living with you." I said solemnly. "Besides, living with you, with a big Caddy to ride around in, who wouldn't want to live forever?"

We drove about ten miles to his apartment. He parked in the basement garage and we took the elevator up to the second floor. It was a new building, and his apartment was elegantly furnished and very comfortable.

Living with David was a completely new experience for me. He was a real gentleman and he treated me very gently and tenderly. After I had been there for a while, he told me quite a lot about himself.

Several times he told me I reminded him of his baby sister. It turned out that she had been killed in a tragic automobile accident when she was only sixteen. I decided maybe that was why he felt so strongly about suicide, since she had lost her life so senselessly. She and David had been very close, apparently, and I often wondered if he had taken me in because he no longer had his sister to shower affection and presents on.

For such a gentle man to have such a strange hobby fascinated me. David's hobby was guns. He had all kinds —antiques, foreign ones, and both rifles and pistols. Every so often, he'd drive me to an old dump outside of town and give me lessons in shooting. The first time I held a gun in my hand, I thought fleetingly of Art and his Bonnie-and-

Clyde gag; but after repeated training, I became a pretty good shot.

David also taught me to drive the Cadillac. He let me use it for errands—to go to the store or the beauty parlor, never very far. It didn't seem to bother him that I had no license and wasn't old enough to get one. I thought that was rather odd, because he was a careful man, but I was so glad to drive around in that big car that I was extra careful so I wouldn't be picked up.

One night when we went out for pizza, I was initiated into David's business. On our way home, I heard an ambulance coming up behind us, with the siren going full blast. David pulled over to the curb promptly, but he didn't stay there. As soon as the ambulance pulled on by, he pulled out behind it. The faster the ambulance went, the faster we went, and I began to get scared.

"David, what are you doing?" I asked.

"Following the ambulance, stupid," he snapped. "Fasten your seat belt and shut up."

I obeyed and hung on to the side of the car as we swerved and swayed through red lights, following the ambulance. Surprisingly, no one stopped us—maybe they thought we were officials.

The driver of the ambulance slammed on the brakes and I peered out at what looked like a head-on collision. David slowed up and pulled over to the side, about a block ahead of the ambulance. He jumped out of the car and joined the crowd on the sidewalk. I didn't know what to do so I joined him.

The crowd inched closer to the accident and we moved along with it. One man was lying on the street near one of the cars; he looked as though he was out cold. The two ambulance attendants put the man on a stretcher, loaded him into the ambulance, and drove off.

As the crowd started to thin out, I noticed a policeman talking to a man near the cracked-up cars. Instead of moving on, David moved closer to the two and stood on the corner, watching and listening intently. The man got into the police car and talked earnestly with the policeman and his partner for a few minutes, and David stayed where he was.

"Why don't we go on home?" I asked.

David ignored me; he remained rooted to the spot where he could see the man and the two policemen. Finally, two wreckers pulled up and started working on the two cars. David pulled out a pad and pencil and started writing busily.

At last the man, who I guessed was the driver of one of the totaled cars, got out of the police car and the policemen drove off. The man spoke to one of the wreckers and stood watching them for a few minutes; then he, too, turned to leave.

David stepped up to him. "Sir, may I introduce myself? I'm David Schwartz. Sure am sorry to see what happened to you. Are you hurt?"

"Not really," the man said, "a bump or two, but thank God that's all. The other guy is really in bad shape. So is my car," he added.

"Looks like it was pretty near totaled," David said.

"Yes, it's pretty well shot. Worst thing is, I've only had the car four weeks."

"Surely the insurance company will take care of it?" David asked.

"Oh, sure—I guess so. It's just that it was a new car, and. . . . " His voice trailed off.

"Well, sir," David said, "I'd like to make a deal with you for your wrecked car."

"My wrecked car? But it isn't worth a cent, except for insurance. I doubt there's even a headlight or wheel cover left whole."

"Yes, but that's on the front end," David said. "All I need is the back end. You see, it just so happens that I have a Riviera just like yours. Last week I stopped at a stop sign and a truck was right on my tail. The driver lost his brakes and he practically pushed my back end right through the front. It's a real mess, but the whole front end, including the motor, is okay. Well, I'm pretty good with cars, and when I saw your accident, I realized the back end was in pretty good shape. I think I could use it. You interested?"

"I might be," the man replied. "I'll talk to my insurance man and maybe we can work out a deal."

David brought out his little pad again and he wrote down the man's name, address, and telephone number. "I'll call you in a few days and we'll see if we can strike up a deal," he said.

The two shook hands and we turned in different directions and walked off. I was dying to find out what David was doing, but after his snappishness over the ambulance-following, I figured I'd better not question him now.

The next morning, as we were eating breakfast, I started to question him. "David, level with me. What's with this accident bit and your buying this guy's car last night?"

"Baby, I told you I had something going for me that you would never believe. Well, I'm not ready to tell you just yet, but you wait a few days and I'll tell you all about it." He picked up his fork and started in on his scrambled eggs.

I reached over and put my hand on his knee. "Please

tell me now," I wheedled. "Come on, you can trust me."

David laid down his fork, reached over, and smacked my hand from his knee. Then he picked up his fork again, finished his breakfast, and walked out of the room without another word. I stayed out of his way the next day, but I heard him talking to the man with the Riviera on the phone. He offered him seven hundred dollars for his demolished car. Apparently the man accepted, as David told him he'd come right over with a check.

"Come on. You can come along with me," he told me.

I was dying of curiosity. None of it made any sense to me, but I *had* to find out what was going on, so I kept my lip buttoned and hopped into the car with David. We drove over to the man's house and I waited in the car while David gave him a check and came back with some papers. From there we went to the license bureau and David told me he was getting the ownership papers transferred to his name.

Next we drove to a junkyard. I waited in the car again while David went into the office. In a few minutes he was back in the car and he told me, "We've got to follow this wrecker to the garage the Riviera was towed to."

We followed the wrecker to a gas station, where he picked up the Riviera, then back to the junkyard. The driver unhooked the car, reached into his pocket, and handed David five twenty-dollar bills. David shook his hand and we got back into the Caddy and drove away.

"I just don't understand you," I said as we drove away. "You gave the owner of the Riviera seven hundred dollars for his car, then you sold it to a junk dealer for one hundred dollars. According to my calculations that makes you out six hundred dollars."

David just smiled.

"Did you or did you not just lose six hundred dollars?" I asked.

"Listen, little girl, the only time I lose money is to make money. You just watch your Uncle David and you'll see. You brought me luck on this deal, so after I finish it up, I'm going to blow you to the best dinner in town," he said. "And you can come along and watch how I do it!"

That evening we drove all round town. David kept looking from one side of the street to the other. After a couple of hours of this, with no conversation, I was about ready to blow up when David spoke up.

"Maybe you can help me," he said. "I'm looking for a new, blue-and-white, Buick Riviera like the one that got cracked up. If you can spot one before I do, I'll buy you two dinners!"

I joined David in looking, as we drove up one street and down the next, but neither of us had any luck. Streaks of dawn were showing before David gave up and we returned to the apartment to fall into bed.

The next night, we went to a neighboring town and repeated the slow cruising up and down, up and down. Again we had no luck—neither of us could find a Riviera that matched. We kept this up for almost a week, going to a different town each night.

One night, I was bleary-eyed from searching when we passed a Buick parking lot. "Wait a minute," I shouted to David, "I think I found one. Isn't that what we're looking for?" I pointed out a car about three rows back from the street.

David pulled over to the curb and looked. "That's it! Good girl. Now we can go home."

I stared at him in disbelief, but home we went and sat and watched the late movie on television. Just as I was getting ready to go to bed, David reached out and took my hand.

"Let's go take one more look at that car," he said.

"Are you crazy? Quit kidding and come to bed. We can take another look in the morning," I said, and started toward the bedroom.

"Becky, we need to go *now,* and I'm not kidding."

I didn't ask any more questions; I knew that tone of voice. There was no sense in arguing, so I got into my coat again and off we went.

David parked a block away from the Buick car lot and explained to me what I was to do.

"Now listen very carefully and do exactly as I tell you," he said. "You sit right here behind the wheel, with the motor idling. If a police car passes you and heads for the lot, put your lights on and drive straight ahead, past the lot a block or so. Get it?"

"Yes, I get it. I'm supposed to be a lookout. But, what are you going to do?"

"I'm going to steal that car, dummy. Now, you keep your eyes wide open, and remember—if a cop car comes along, just put on the lights and drive straight ahead. If you don't keep awake and listen carefully, you and I are liable to be dining on beans and bread in jail the next couple of nights, instead of out on the town as I promised. It's up to you."

David got out and unlocked the trunk. He came back with some kind of contraption in his hand.

"What's that?" I asked.

"It's what they call a 'toy.' It's the mechanism that I use to pull out the lock system from the steering column. See that system?" David pointed to the steering column of the Cadillac. "Well, it's supposed to be steal-proof, but this little pulley bypasses all that. All I have to do is push it in, give a couple of little twists, and pull out the whole steal-proof mechanism. I can bypass the ignition system and start the car up on my own."

I just gaped. I knew nothing about the innards or mechanisms of a car, so, as David walked toward the lot, I got behind the wheel of the Cadillac and looked thoughtfully at the steering column. I started the motor and looked ahead and behind. Headlights showed in the rear-vision mirror and my heart thudded but, as the car pulled abreast, I saw it wasn't a police car.

A few more cars passed by, but it was late and not an hour when many cars were on the streets. Finally, I saw David drive out of the lot in the Riviera, so I followed him home.

He pulled over to the curb and came over to me. "I'm going to put the Riviera in my parking space in the garage for the night," he said. "You park the Caddy here and we'll move it in the morning. I want that Buick on ice for delivery tomorrow."

I did as he instructed, but I was pretty nervous. When I got up to the apartment, David was getting ready for bed.

"How can you be as cool as a cucumber?" I asked. "Aren't you afraid of getting caught? I know I'll never sleep a wink tonight."

David laughed. "Relax, baby. I've been doing this for two years and I've never been caught yet. Besides, we won't have that Riviera long enough to get caught. Come on and get some shut-eye."

Early next morning David made several phone calls. I heard him dickering over prices and he finally agreed to deliver for three thousand dollars. Someone was getting a fantastic price on a new car, I knew, and I also knew that we would have a lot of money, but my stomach just wouldn't quiet down. I was still so nervous I was shaking.

"Come on," David said. "We've got a lot to do. I promised delivery for this afternoon."

He took a pair of license plates out of the closet and we left. I watched him switch the plates on the Riviera, then he got in and drove for several hours to a small town in upstate New York. I followed him in the Cadillac.

We parked in front of a restaurant, went in, and sat down at a table by the window. In a few moments a man, who turned out to be the restaurant owner, came over and joined us.

"Look out the window. There's your car," David said.

"Hey, that's a beauty!"

"Brand, spanking new," David said proudly.

"Come on back to my office," the man said. "I'll pay you there." We followed him through several doors to a small office in the back. The owner reached into a drawer and pulled out a checkbook.

"Oh, no," David said. "No checks. Remember I said a cash deal?"

"But I don't have that much cash on me."

David rose. "No deal, then. Sorry, but it's cold, hard cash, or nothing."

"Now wait a minute, be reasonable," the man said. "My check is good. If you want to, call the bank from here and they'll guarantee you I have a balance to cover it."

"I don't want to be unreasonable," David said. "It depends on how badly you want the car. If you bought it from a dealer, it would cost you at least six thousand dollars, so you can't blame me for wanting cash.

"Here's an idea. My girl and I will sit right here in this

office and *you* go to the bank and get the money—better yet, we'll follow you in the car and wait for you. How's that for being reasonable?"

The man thought for a moment, then he said, "Well, that sounds okay. You drive me over and I'll get the cash for you. Wait a minute while I tell the waitress I'll be gone a few minutes."

"Just to show you I trust you, I'll leave the Buick here," David said. "When you give me the cash, I'll give you the keys."

As we followed the man to the bank in the Caddy, I thought of something. "David, if you had those keys all the time, why did you have to use that 'toy' to start the Riv with?" I asked.

"I didn't, silly. This morning, while you and I were still fast asleep in bed, my friend Burt, the locksmith, came over and made keys for it. I paid him about one hundred dollars for his time."

The man in front of us pulled over to the curb and we stopped, too. He was gone for only a few minutes and, when he came out, David swung open the back door of the Caddy. David turned around and the man handed him a roll of bills. As David counted, I counted, to myself, along with him—thirty one-hundred-dollar bills—three thousand dollars!

David reached into the glove compartment and pulled out some papers, which he handed over. "Here are your papers. As you'll see, I've signed the car over to you. All you have to do is go to the license bureau and get new plates and registration."

"How about a receipt for the sale of the car?"

"I don't have a receipt—although I did include a bill of sale, along with the legal papers. That's all you need. You have the car; I have the money. That's the way I do business."

Well, okay, so long as it's all legal."

"Why, of course it's all legal," David said indignantly. He put his hand in his pocket. "If you don't want it, let's forget about it and I'll sell the car to someone else."

"Oh, no, no—don't do that. I don't want to mess up the deal. I'm perfectly satisfied."

The two shook hands, David handed him the keys, and we drove off.

On the drive back, I was quiet. My mind was going lickety-split, trying to fit pieces of the puzzle together. I knew that David got his money stealing cars, but fitting in all the details was more than I could manage.

"Come on, David," I said. "I know what's been going on the past few days and weeks, but there are still some pieces missing. Fill me in. Just how do you manage it all?"

David was feeling expansive. "Sure," he said. "It's really all very simple—mostly a question of biding your time and keeping your eyes open, as you saw. Once you locate a totaled car, it's easy to get the owner to sell. Once he sells, you get the registration papers for a new car. Then you locate one exactly like it and steal it. If you're smart, you have a list of likely customers that you keep up-to-date. The only ones who are stupid are the customers. They check the year, the model, the make of car, but very few of them have enough sense to check the serial numbers, which would blow the whole thing.

"Of course, in my time," he added, "I have even changed the serial numbers, but only if the customer inquired. The poor dope is running around in a hot car and has no comeback if the police ever check it out. It's very seldom that the police do, I might add."

From that time on, whenever our funds got a little low, we kept on the lookout for accidents. And David kept playing his game with me—if I located a matching car first, he took me out to dinner. I got so good at spotting them that, at one time, he owed me five dinners!

Then one night, when we were cruising around looking for a Pontiac, David said, "There's a police car tailing us, Becky. Don't look around."

He kept watching through the rearview mirror as we picked up a little speed. We stayed within the speed limit, but in a minute, the siren and red lights came on. David pulled over to the curb and stopped.

Two policeman walked up to us. One politely asked for David's registration, while the other peered into the backseat. David handed over the registration and asked, "What is it you guys are looking for?"

"We're checking for drugs," one replied.

"Do I look like a drug addict—or my girl? We have no drugs," David said indignantly.

"Will you both please get out of the car?" The policeman looked under the seat; he checked the glove compartment, the sun visors, and under the carpeting.

In the meantime, the other officer had taken the keys out of the ignition and was opening the trunk. He reached in and pulled out the "toy."

"Young man, what do you call this?"

"A pulley," David said.

"Oh, it's a pulley, is it? Well, do you have a permit that authorizes you to carry this pulley?"

David pulled out his wallet and started to fumble through it. The policeman waited.

"I guess I must have left it home. Maybe, if . . . ." David stuttered.

"I think you and the young lady had better come down to the station house with us, right now," the officer interrupted. He pulled a pair of handcuffs from his hip, pushed David's hands behind his back, and locked him up. The other officer did the same to me. Then they shoved us into the backseat of the police car, and we drove off.

The handcuffs hurt and I was scared out of my wits. I looked at David, but he didn't seem to be much help. I started to cry.

As we got out of the car at the station house, David said, "Listen, Officer, this young girl with me is just out on a date. She had nothing to do with any of this. Why don't you let her go?"

"We'll have to book both of you. If it turns out the girl had nothing to do with you, she'll be released."

As soon as we got inside, they led David into another room. A matron came in, searched me, and removed the handcuffs. Then she took me to be fingerprinted. By the time they brought David back into the same room, I was ready to confess to anything—even murder—but I couldn't stop crying long enough to answer the few questions the matron asked me.

David gave me the barest of glances and said, "Just tell the truth, kid—that we were out on a date and you don't know anything. You'll be okay."

An officer led me into another office and asked me a few questions. "How long have you known David Schwartz? What were you doing when we picked you up?"

Remembering David's advice, I stuck to his story. "I've only been out with him a few times. He seems to be a nut about cars; sometimes we'd go to a movie or a pizza place, but mostly we just drove around looking at cars."

The officer sighed. "All right, I'll accept that answer.

Schwartz has admitted his guilt, but he swears you are innocent and know nothing about it. You're free to leave. Do you want someone to take you home?"

"Oh, no, I'll be all right, thank you," I replied. I didn't want to go back to my folks' place and I was afraid if they drove me to David's they'd know I'd been lying.

As I walked down the long hallway, I saw David sitting on a chair. He didn't look up. I so wanted to say something to him, to pat him or ruffle his hair, but I didn't dare. He was a gentleman to the end, in protecting me, and I didn't want to spoil things for him or for me. I opened the outside door, turned and gave a little flick of my hand toward him, then moved on out to the sidewalk.

When I got back to David's apartment, I sat and thought for a long time. This had been almost like a real home to me, but I knew I had to leave or David might get into more trouble if the cops found me here. I had no idea what would happen to David, but I knew I was going to have to hit the road again, so I toured the apartment looking for any money or small objects I might hock if I got broke.

7

It didn't take me long to hitch a ride to the East Village in New York City. The East Village is one of the most notorious places in the world for addicts, alcoholics, pimps, prostitutes—you name it, you can find it in the East Village. Although mugging and stealing—even murder—is a way of life here, it is a Mecca for runaways.

I wound up on Twelfth Street between Avenues A and B, and surprisingly enough nothing happened to me as I strolled along. My purse was draped over my shoulder, but no one tried to snatch it; no one hit me on the head. I saw quite a few addicts hanging loose, but none of them paid any attention to me.

As it began to get dark as usual I started to worry about where I'd spend the night. Then I spotted a girl of about twenty-five, leaning against a building. I was sure she was a prostitute, but there was something about her that made me trust her immediately, and I did need a place to stay.

"Excuse me," I said flatly. "I'm a runaway and I need a place to spend the night. Can you help me out?"

She smiled, then broke into a big laugh. "Baby," she said, "I know where you can get a free room at the Hilton."

"You mean *the* Hilton? Isn't that way uptown?" I asked.

"Well, it may not be *the* Hilton you're thinking about, but you can stay with me, at what we locals call the Hilton."

"Okay, fine. I'd appreciate that," I said.

We walked about a block and stopped in front of a vacant tenement house. It sure wasn't the Hilton I was thinking of! Part of it was burned out, and all of the windows were broken; some were boarded up, some gaped open. We entered a long hallway and the strong smell of urine hit my nostrils. It was almost overpowering, but I clenched my teeth and followed my benefactor. As my eyes got accustomed to the dim light filtering in from outside, I could see the graffiti—mostly four-letter words —covering the walls.

"Look out for the third step; it's not there," my friend instructed as she started up the stairway at the end of the hall.

I put my hand on the railing to balance myself, as I tried to skip the step, and almost fell to the hallway below. The banister swayed back and forth as I clutched at it.

"Sorry about that," the girl said, "I forgot to tell you that most of the supports are gone for the railing."

We made it to the second floor safely and I turned to my still unknown friend. "I forgot to ask your name," I said. "Mine is Becky."

"Martha," she said. "Now walk kind of softly along here. Watch that ceiling overhead. Last week a chunk came loose and just missed my head."

I looked upward toward where she was pointing and saw gaping holes; there were more holes than plaster left. The walls, too, were almost down to the lathing.

Martha led me down the hall to a room with a door. We stepped inside and I could make out mattresses scattered around the floor. In one corner a boy and girl lay in a tight clinch, kissing each other as if it were going out of style.

Our entrance was ignored by both of them.

"Welcome, Becky," Martha said wryly. "You can have any mattress you want."

She must have seen the shock and disbelief on my face —the place was even worse than where I'd stayed in San Francisco—because she added, "Now, you don't really *have* to stay here tonight, but the only other free place I know of is about four blocks away. It's Lincoln Park and you can sleep on one of the park benches, provided a wino doesn't beat you to it. Of course, the last time I knew of a girl sleeping there, she was raped by a group of fellas. But you take your chances and you make your choice."

I gulped and said weakly, "Thanks. I think I'll stay here tonight. By the way, where is the bathroom?"

Martha gave a short laugh. "The bathroom? It's down at the very end of the hall. Just follow your nose; there's no running water. Most of us use the subway or other public rest rooms except in dire emergencies."

I started down the hallway and soon realized what she had meant when she said, "Follow your nose." The closer I got to the closed door at the end of the hall, the stronger the stench became. I opened the door and closed it again quickly; the filth and smell were unbelievable and for a few minutes I thought I was going to throw up.

Martha was watching from the doorway of the room, but she said nothing about my quick return, just led me over to a mattress and by gestures indicated that I could use that one. I threw myself down on it and tried to get my thoughts organized so I could get some sleep. I got little, as girls kept drifting in and out all night long.

The next morning Martha bought me breakfast at a small Spanish restaurant on the corner, where we freshened up in the rest room. The owners, a friendly couple, seemed used to their customers washing up as well as eating.

After we ate, Martha asked if I had anything in particular to do. When I said no, she asked if I'd like to go on an errand with her, and I accepted.

We took a subway up to the Bronx, and after we walked up to street level, Martha asked me to wait on the corner for her. I was a little nervous, as I didn't like the looks of the people around, but there was nothing else to do, since she obviously did not want me to come farther with her.

Martha returned in about ten minutes carrying a small package under her arm. She said nothing, just hooked her arm in mine and marched me back to the subway entrance. We got off the subway in midtown Manhattan and walked up to Forty-Eighth Street to a big hotel. Martha motioned me to a chair in the lobby and took an elevator upstairs.

In a few minutes she got off another elevator, without the package, and walked over to where I was sitting.

"Come on, let's go," she said, and again we headed for the subway.

This time we got off in the Village again, but on the west side. Martha steered me into a very nice-looking restaurant, and we both sat down.

"Getting hungry?" Martha asked. Then she smiled. "Let's have a steak. How do you like yours?"

"Oh, boy," I said, "steak! I'll have mine rare."

After she had ordered for both of us, I turned to her and asked, "Martha, what are you up to? Where did you get the money for a restaurant like this? And what was that mysterious package you picked up and delivered? Come on, level with me."

Martha gave a funny little laugh. "Okay, Becky, I'll

level with you. Once in a while I make a run, for which I get paid five hundred dollars. It scares me each time I do it; I imagine people following me, winding up in jail— all sorts of things. So, this time I decided to ask you to come along and keep me company. You didn't mind?"

"No, I didn't mind at all. But what do you mean— making a run?"

Martha leaned over and whispered, "A run is carrying drugs from one place to another."

"You mean to tell me—" I was aghast, and my face must have shown it for Martha shushed me and said, "We'll talk about it later."

We returned to the tenement and Martha led me to a room down the hall from where we were staying. She pulled out a needle she had stashed behind the baseboard, and we both got off. I knew the procedure since I had watched two groups get off at the pad I stayed at in San Francisco.

We returned to the street corner in a little while, and a man came up to us.

"How would you two girls like to stay in a nice, free apartment?" he asked.

Martha challenged him. "What do you mean? Don't you know who you're talking to? Have you ever heard of Mayor Connelly?"

The man nodded.

"Well," Martha continued, shaking her finger in his face for emphasis, "I'm his daughter and this young lady is my cousin. We are doing some survey work on the Lower East Side so we can clean this place up, and we think we've figured out a good way to do it."

"Get rid of the junkies and runaways?" the man asked. And before Martha could reply, he continued, "Listen, girlie, don't try to kid me. See that furniture store down the street?"

He pointed down the block, and Martha and I looked obediently. "I own that store and I've been here for more than twenty-six years. I know everything that goes on in this block. For instance, you hang out on this street corner and you've lived in that burned-out tenement across the street for quite some time. This young lady, however, just came on the block a few days ago. Right?"

He seemed to know everything and didn't want any answers, so I just nodded my head.

"I'm not playing games with you," he said. "I'm giving you a break. Now, listen. Every so often junkies break into my store and walk off with half the place. All I want you to do is stay in the nice, clean, two-bedroom apartment above the store and let me know when someone breaks in. You don't have to try to stop them, or handcuff them, or even yell at them. All I want you to do is call me on the phone. I'll take it from there. How about it?"

"Now, exactly why have you chosen Becky and me to help you?" Martha asked.

"That's easy. You're both junkies, and I figure if both of you live upstairs, your junkie friends here in the street won't knock off the place. Right?"

Martha smiled. I was sure she knew the man was right. I shrugged my shoulders at her. What did we have to lose?

"It's a deal," she said, and the two shook hands.

"My name is Johnson," the man said. He reached into his pocket and pulled out a key and handed it to Martha. "You might as well move in right now, and spread the word around as fast as you can."

"Don't worry, we will," Martha replied, and we hurried to the tenement to pick up our few belongings. "That guy is up to something," she said to me as we walked up the steps.

"Well, what do we have to lose?" I asked. "At least we'll have our own bathroom, and he said it has two bedrooms!"

Martha turned the key in the lock and we walked into a lovely apartment. We both stood stock-still and admired the furnishings; they were serviceable, but very attractive. I walked on into the nearest bedroom and let out a yell for Martha.

"Look, there's a pair of men's shoes under the bed," I told her as she ran in.

"Relax," she said, "maybe Mr. Johnson forgot them."

I jerked open the closet door—it was full of men's clothes. "You may be right; this guy is up to something," I said. "His clothes are all here. Why didn't he tell us?"

Just then we heard the apartment door open. We both ran to the bedroom door and watched as a young man walked in. He glanced at us with no curiosity and walked on into the kitchen.

Martha and I stared at each other. "We'd better find out what gives here," Martha said, and we both headed for the kitchen.

"I'm Martha and this is Becky. *We* are taking this apartment over now, at Mr. Johnson's request. Who are you?"

The man turned from the open refrigerator door and gave us the once-over. He still didn't say anthing.

"Well, say something," I shouted at him in exasperation. "Who are you and what are you doing here?"

The young man took out a beer, closed the door, and went to the cupboard for a glass. Then he sat down at the kitchen table and calmly poured himself a glass of beer and drank it, still saying nothing. From the way he acted right at home, I knew the clothes in the bedroom must be his, but I still didn't know where he fit in.

Martha sat down at the table with him. "What's the matter with you? Can't you talk?" she asked.

He put down his glass and burst into a torrent of words. The only trouble was they were all in a foreign language, and we couldn't understand a word he said. Finally, after many gestures back and forth from all of us, he got out, "Me, Lars."

I started to laugh; I couldn't help it, all I could think of was Tarzan, and I wanted to say, "Me, Jane." Martha finally broke down, too, and even Lars joined in the laughter. He seemed harmless enough, so we decided to let things ride until the following day when we could check with Mr. Johnson.

It turned out he was Mr. Johnson's nephew from Sweden, and he worked in the furniture store. Mr Johnson assured us that Lars was a good boy and would not trouble us and asked us not to tell anyone he was upstairs with us. He said that Lars was in the country illegally and couldn't get citizenship papers, so he hauled furniture and kept the place clean to earn his keep.

Martha and I were perfectly happy with the other bedroom, and as the days went by we taught Lars a sort of Pidgin English so we could understand each other better. We spread the word on the street that Mr. Johnson was a friend of ours and the store was to be let alone while we lived there. In all the time we were there, we never heard a sound, and the breaking and entering stopped after we moved in.

The days passed quickly enough; whenever money was getting short Martha would make another run and I would accompany her. Lars kept pretty much to himself, and we saw him only occasionally. One night, Mr. Johnson approached us as we were going into the apartment and asked us out to dinner. We agreed and he took us to a nice Italian Place on Twelfth Street off Fifth Avenue.

As we were dawdling over coffee, Mr. Johnson turned to Martha and asked, "How do you like my nephew, Lars?"

"He's a nice guy," she said. "He keeps to himself pretty much and hasn't given us any trouble. We don't talk much but he always gives us a great big smile. Why do you ask?"

"Well, Lars and I have a problem. He doesn't want to go back to Sweden and he can't keep working for me illegally much longer. I'd always hoped I could turn the business over to Lars, eventually; I have no children or family of my own," he said.

"Turn it over to me," I said, and grinned. "I'll be a daughter to you."

Mr. Johnson didn't think that was funny. He stared me down until my eyes dropped to the table.

"I've come up with a solution, I think," he said to Martha, "Do you think you could love Lars?"

"Love him? Are you kidding? I don't even know him, and how could I love a guy I can't even talk to?"

"I think *I* could love him," I interrupted.

Again Mr. Johnson ignored me and went on talking to Martha. "You know if you and Lars got married, he could get citizenship papers through you and he wouldn't have to go back to Sweden."

Martha bridled. "Now listen. You're a nice guy. You gave us a nice apartment. Lars is a nice guy. But marrying him wasn't part of the bargain."

"How much would it be worth to you?" Mr. Johnson asked.

"What do you mean, how much is it worth to me?"

"I'll give you three hundred dollars cash to marry Lars. It would mean being a wife in name only; don't worry about that. All you'd have to do is marry him and sign some papers that would help him get citizenship through being married to an American. Sound like a good deal?"

Martha continued to look nonplussed for a minute or two. Then she looked over at me and gave me a funny little grin. I guessed she was going to accept the offer.

"You make it five hundred dollars and you may pronounce Lars and me husband and wife," she said

"It's a deal." Mr. Johnson reached into his coat pocket and pulled out a wad of bills. He peeled off ten twenties and handed them to Martha. "Here's two hundred dollars. You get the other three hundred dollars after the marriage and the papers are all legal."

Martha took the money, put it in her purse, and we all left the restaurant.

The next day I went with Lars and Martha while they got their blood tests, and three days later we went to City Hall for the license. They were married there and after the ceremony, Lars took Martha and me out for dinner.

A few days later Mr. Johnson went with Lars and Martha and they signed the necessary papers that Lars needed to apply for citizenship. When Martha came home alone, I knew from the smirk on her face that she had gotten the additional three hundred dollars.

All this time, our living arrangements continued as before. It was evident that Lars was content to consider his marriage to Martha strictly a business deal.

A few weeks after the marriage, Martha and I came

home one afternoon and discovered that our key wouldn't work on the door. We went downstairs and told Mr. Johnson.

"I know," he said. "I changed the lock at noon, while you were out. Come here, I want to show you something."

I stared at the piece of plywood he pointed to. It was fitted over a broken window of the shop.

He began to shout. "This is the thanks I get for giving you a roof over your heads. Your friends came back last night and broke in again. Our deal is over. I should have known no junkie could be trusted. Now get out of here before I call the cops."

Martha tried to protest, but he pushed us right on out the door and locked it after us, screaming filth at us all the while.

Martha and I looked at each other forlornly. We hadn't had anything to do with the break-in, but it was obvious Mr. Johnson wasn't going to believe us.

Finally, I realized we couldn't stand there forever, so I turned to Martha with a small smile and asked, "Ever been to Florida?"

She attempted a weak smile in return, took my hand, and we started walking down the street. "Southland, here we come," I said.

8

We were lucky and got to Florida in just a couple of days. We slept on the beaches the first few nights, until I ran into Erlene, a girl from home. Erlene gave me some news that shook me up a bit—she said my dad had left home and was living with another woman. I wondered fleetingly how my mom was making out, but Erlene got on to other subjects and I never did find out.

Erlene took Martha and me home with her and introduced us to a bunch of kids who were all living together in a great big house. She told me several of the kids had some money or picked some up from time to time, and they all agreed that Martha and I could stay with them. Martha wasn't too crazy about the idea—I guessed it was because she was older than the rest of us—but I talked her into it and she was a good sport about everything. After a few days, she picked up a part-time job in a store downtown, and I ran with the pack of kids more and more.

It turned out they were all hard drinkers and most of them were out-and-out alcoholics. It didn't surprise me too much, as there were a lot of kids at home who were as addicted to alcohol as the junkies were to drugs.

Some nights we'd have supper and drink on the beach; others we'd go to a pizza place or a bar and stay until the place closed up. I liked being part of the gang, but I was a lot of trouble to them since many of the places wouldn't let me in because I was underage.

One night we were sitting at the dining-room table at home, eating pizza, when Erlene said, "Does anybody have an expired driver's license for Becky?"

I looked at her in astonishment, but before I could question her, the girl sitting across the table spoke up, "My friend Tina has one, I think. She's about Becky's size. Why don't I give her a ring?"

"You do that, right now," Erlene told her.

The girl went into the other room and I could hear her dialing. A few minutes later she came back.

"Yes, she's home. She said if you drop by her place, she'll give it to you." She gave Erlene directions on how to get to her friend's house.

I tagged along with Erlene, having no idea what they were talking about. "Erlene, what are you up to?" I asked.

"I'm getting you the identification you need so you won't be hassled at the bars all the time."

"How can you do that?"

"It's simple. We're picking up an expired driver's license from someone who is about the same height as you and has the same color hair."

It still wasn't clear to me, but I shut up as Erlene pulled up to a house. She walked up to the door, rang the bell, and talked to a girl for a few minutes. The girl handed her something, which Erlene examined, then flipped her hand and returned to the car.

We drove back to the house and I followed Erlene into her bedroom. She pulled out a typewriter from a closet, took an ink eraser and carefully erased the date on the license, then typed in a new one. She handed the license to me.

"There you are. There's your driver's license. All you have to do is memorize the information on that license and you're all set," Erlene told me.

I examined the license carefully. My name was now Tina Commack; my address was 1335 Prefect Street, Fort Lauderdale, Florida. I was five-foot-two, blue-eyed and had brown hair. And suddenly I had become two years older!

When we walked back into the dining room, most of the gang had gone out, so I had to wait until the next night to try out the new scheme. That night we all went to a popular bar we'd been to before. As we walked toward the front entrance, I saw the bouncer—big as a mountain— standing there, checking IDs. I started to turn around and go back.

"What's the matter with you?" Bernard asked.

"That bouncer. He's turned me down so many times, he'll never let me in tonight, new driver's license or not. He'll recognize me."

"You must be kidding," Bernard said. "You watch; he'll let you in."

He took me by the arm and we both approached the bouncer. In a bored voice, he asked to see Bernard's identification. Bernard flipped out his driver's license and the bouncer waved him on in the door. Erlene pushed past me and showed hers; he waved her on by. Then he came to me.

"Well, if it isn't the sweet little old lady again," he said.

My heart dropped into my shoes: I knew he'd recognized me; now I'd never get in.

"May I please see your identification?" he asked in a falsetto voice, with a big grin on his face.

I reached into my purse, pulled out the altered driver's license, handed it to him, and held my breath. The bouncer looked at it, then he grinned again. "You're just the little old lady we've been waiting for. Welcome to the Troubadour Bar," he said, and waved me grandiosely through the door.

I scooted through the door and said to Bernard breathlessly, "Can you beat that? Just the other night, he actually shook me for trying to get in because I was under age. Tonight he treats me like his mother. I can't figure him out."

"Oh, forget it," Bernard said. "That ape doesn't care how old you are. You know, I know, and *he* knows that you're not eighteen years old. But now you've got a driver's license that says you're eighteen, and if the cops bust this place, the bouncer is protected. He did his job and checked you out. Don't worry about him any more."

I didn't. I had three sloe gin fizzes that night and felt like a real big shot, sitting up at the bar! From that time on, I think I enjoyed showing my proof of age more than I did the actual drinking.

One night not long after that, a bunch of us were drinking on the beach, when along came the cops and hauled us in for drunkenness. I was pretty drunk and didn't remember much of what happened when they first took me to jail, but when I came to, I found myself in a dank cell alone.

I was frantic to let Martha know where I was, as I was sure she could get me out since she was older and had a job for security. I asked several of the guards, but most of them just laughed at me. One of them tried to make a pass at me and I told him off.

Finally, one guard let himself into the cell with a key. "What seems to be the trouble, young lady?" he asked. "You seem to be pretty worked up over something."

I told him about wanting to get in touch with Martha

and he said he'd do what he could to locate her. Bill was different from the other guards. He was very gentle and made no wisecracks. He leaned against the door of the cell and asked me questions about myself; he said he had a daughter my age and it hurt him to see a kid like me drunk and in jail.

When I told him I was a runaway, he shook his head and began to talk about Jesus, and about His love for all of us. Bill told me I thought I was running away from home—from my parents, maybe even from myself—but actually I was running away from Jesus.

"Open your heart and let Jesus in," he told me. "You'll be a better girl for it."

When he left me, I thought about what he had said and I knew he was right. I was scared and lonely and homesick, and I wished so for Jesus' love for myself that I wept.

A few hours later Bill returned to my cell with a big grin on his face. "Good news, you're getting out," he said.

He opened the cell door and led me down the hall, and there in the doorway stood Martha with a big smile on her face.

"She's making bail for you," Bill said. "See, someone loves you! And don't you forget what I told you, either; Jesus will always love you." He gave me a pat on the shoulder and nudged me toward Martha.

I started toward her, then turned and ran back to Bill and gave him a great big hug. He hugged me back, then gently disengaged himself and walked on back toward the cells.

"What was all that hugging and kissing about?" Martha asked as we walked out of the jail.

"There was something different about him," I began. "He . . . ."

"Well, what was different about that cop? To me, a cop is a cop. They're all alike."

"Funny thing," I said slowly, "I never really did think of him as a cop. The difference is. . . . "

"What was the difference?" Martha asked impatiently.

"The difference is Jesus."

"Jesus?" Martha's voice was incredulous. "What's gotten into you? You mean to tell me you've got religion all of a sudden?"

"Well, not exactly." It was difficult to put into words, I found. "I just discovered what happens when Jesus is *really* real and lives within a person. There is a love and concern no one can describe and I could tell it was really felt."

"You mean to tell me *you* felt this whatever-you-call-it—this Jesus' love?"

"Yes, I really felt it when Bill was talking to me. And I still feel some now."

"Man, you've really flipped," Martha said, and she kept a tight-lipped silence all the way back to the house.

When the gang saw me walk in, they cheered. I looked around at them resentfully. "I thought all you guys were busted, too," I said. "What are you doing here?"

"We were busted," Erlene replied. "But Bernard wired his parents for the money to get us out. While he was picking it up, someone from the jail called Martha and she told us she'd take care of you."

That evening the others went to a pizza joint to celebrate, but I went to bed early. I was still disturbed by Bill and his love for Jesus. Would Jesus really love someone like me? I felt haunted.

The next day Martha said she wanted to talk to me, so I walked to the store with her.

"Becky," she told me, "I'm quitting today and going back to New York. I kind of miss the Lower East Side and the action there. These kids are a little juvenile for me. I've got enough for plane fare for both of us, if you want to come along."

I was taken aback; I had gotten used to having Martha there when I needed her. But I also liked living the free life with the kids here in Florida.

"Do you really want me to go back with you?" I asked.

"In a way I do, yes. But you're probably better off here. You've made a lot of friends, and there's always Bernard and his family to fall back on if you get into difficulties."

I went to the airport with her the next day and wished her well. I knew I would miss her.

For the next few days and nights I ran around with the crowd, but I was lonely and unsure underneath. I missed Martha more than I had realized I would, and thoughts of Bill and of Jesus interfered with the fun I used to have. I decided I'd better head back north, so I said good-bye to the crowd and thanked them.

Bernard took me to the edge of town and I got out of the car and waved good-bye to him. Then I stuck out my thumb to a car going north, and it stopped right away.

I couldn't get over my good luck, but I had a funny feeling in my stomach when the two girls and boys in the car told me they had been saved and that Jesus had made life worth living. As I listened to them talk about Jesus and how much He loved me and wanted to change my life, I didn't say a word, but I wondered if it was fate that had made this particular group pick me up.

They were very happy companions, and they had a special glow about them. They reminded me of Bill, the guard.

I hated to see them go whèn they dropped me off, but they were hardly out of sight when a car with Louisiana license plates stopped and picked me up. A couple named Hobart were on their way to New England, they told me, and I wasn't much surprised to learn that they, too, were real Christians. They were a lovely couple and were very kind to me. When they stopped for supper, they bought mine, and they included me in the grace they said over the food before we ate. It made me feel wonderful to be included, and again I wondered if it was fate. When they told me I could ride along with them as far as I wanted, I began to think that Jesus was at last looking after *me*.

9

The Hobarts let me off right near the New Jersey Turnpike. We parted with best wishes and regrets on both sides. I got on the turnpike with some trepidation for, while it is an easy place to get a ride—the drivers on the turnpike seem to want companionship more than most—it is loaded with cops watching for hitchhikers.

I saw a brown car approaching and stuck out my thumb. It stopped right beside me, and I yanked open the door and was halfway in before I realized the driver was a state policeman. (He was in uniform, but the car was what is called a "sneaker" car—it bore no police insignia of any kind.) I jerked back and tried to run, but a hand reached out and grabbed me.

"Hold it, young lady," the officer said. He reached back with his other hand and opened the rear door. "Hop in," he commanded.

I obeyed immediately.

"Any identification?" he asked.

I didn't want to show him my forged driver's license, so I said, "No, sir, not on me."

"Just what I expected."

"What do you mean?" I asked, trying to act innocent. "I was on my way to visit relatives in Plainfield and didn't expect to be gone long, so I didn't bring any identification. I didn't think I'd need any."

"I've heard that story dozens of times. Could you please

tell me—without too much of a hassle—what you were really planning?" he asked.

"I was just on my way to my aunt's house, officer."

My voice started to quaver. I wanted to tell him the truth—that I was on my way home to see if I could make up with my folks—but I was sure he'd never believe me.

"Take it easy," he said. "I'll have to bring you in and give your parents a call. You look like a runaway to me, and not a very old one at that."

"But officer. . . . " I protested. This wasn't the way I wanted to go home—to have my mom pick me up at the police station. I wanted to walk into the house under my own steam; I wanted to tell her about Jesus; I wanted to help her and I knew I needed someone to help me. I really started to bawl.

By the time we got to the police station, I had control of myself and I knew this officer wasn't to be fooled, so I gave him my right name and address and telephone number. He came back in a few minutes and said that he had spoken to my mother and she was coming to pick me up.

He took me back to a cell and apologized that there wasn't any other place where he could put me to wait. The officer wasn't a bad guy at all; he made me think a little of Bill. And here I was in another cold, dank cell! I didn't seem to learn much.

Fortunately, Mom showed up before too long and we drove off together. This time, we had little to say to each other on the way home. I don't know how she felt, but I couldn't get the words together to tell her what I felt, and I didn't want to burst out crying again.

After we got into the house, Mom told me to go wash up and said she'd fix us some coffee. When I walked into the kitchen, she poured two cups of coffee and waved me into a kitchen chair.

"Listen, Becky," she said. "It's too late tonight to talk much; we'll save that till morning. I'm sure you're tired and I know I am. But you've got to promise me one thing: not to run away again. I had to guarantee the state police that you wouldn't be picked up again, before they'd let you go."

"I promise, Mom, and—"

"Tomorrow morning is time enough for talking," she said, and got up and headed toward her bedroom. "Get yourself a good night's sleep and I'll see you then."

I came down around ten the next morning. Mom was sitting in the kitchen, and she bounced up and said, "I made you a batch of fresh biscuits this morning. How about some scrambled eggs to go with them?"

I was so astonished that I let fly, before I remembered all my thoughts of Jesus and love. "Why the good-mother act so early in the morning?" I asked. "I haven't had anything but cold cereal that I fixed myself, in the last six or seven years, I guess."

Mom kept stirring the eggs with a fork, but two big tears fell in the frying pan. I waited for her to rail back at me, but she just took out the eggs, added some biscuits, and brought the full plate over to me.

She sat down next to me and gave a big sigh. "I know I have made a lot of mistakes," she said, "both as a mother and as a wife. I tried my best but I just didn't know how or what to do. I didn't tell you, but your father left me some time ago, and I've had lots of time to think."

"I know," I interrupted. "I bumped into Erlene in Florida and she told me he was living with another woman.

"I'm sorry about that, Mom, I truly am," I said awkwardly. "I hope I didn't have anything to do with his leaving."

She sighed again. "It was a lot of things, Becky. I don't know just which one or if it was any one in particular. Everything just piled up. But I haven't given up yet. I've been doing a lot of thinking and a lot of praying, too. Aunt Bessie and Uncle Carl out in Ohio have been a big help to me in furnishing moral support. Do you remember them?"

Yes, I remembered them. They used to live near us and we had seen a lot of them then. I had visited them in Ohio a couple of times, too, when their children were still at home, and I'd always enjoyed them.

"They think maybe visiting them would be a good way for you to sort out your thoughts—without me picking at you, as Aunt Bessie says." Mom gave a little laugh. "Their children are all grown and gone now and they've got that big house, and I suspect they could use some help on the farm, too. What do you think?"

The more I thought about the idea, the more it appealed to me. I agreed to go, so Mom called and made arrangements at the airport. We called Aunt Bessie, Mom's sister, and she sounded happy to have me come, so three days later I left for Ohio.

I recognized Aunt Bessie and Uncle Carl as soon as I stepped off the plane in Cleveland. They were older, of course, but they had a certain glow about them—the "Jesus glow," I realized later—that they had always had, and they seemed genuinely glad to see me.

It was a long drive to their two-hundred-acre farm, and I enjoyed the scenery on the country roads we drove through. It was the end of the summer and the cornfields were beautiful. Uncle Carl told me they had a lot of corn to harvest for their cattle, and he expected some help from me.

Life on the farm did something for me. Working with the cattle, the tractors, and the silage machines was all so different from what I had done with my life so far. I felt I was contributing, and I felt content. Nights, I was so tired physically that I crawled into bed early, but I enjoyed the big farm breakfasts Aunt Bessie fixed almost at the crack of dawn.

We did everything together; it was a new experience for me. They laughed, but gently, when we played Scrabble in the evenings; my vocabulary left a great deal to be desired and they always beat me, but I never minded because they were so considerate and they tried to help me. We prayed together, but somehow I was not yet ready to accept Jesus' love.

Uncle Carl was fattening up one of his prize pigs for the county fair and he told me all the work that had to be done before we could go: the corn had to be gotten in and the silos and bins filled.

Occasionally, I had a note from my mother and sometimes she called. Each time, I felt a little closer to her, and I had enough sense now to tell her so. Communication was one thing I was learning from Aunt Bessie and Uncle Carl —they shared every thought, and I never heard a cross word between them. Consideration and caring were important to them, too: each of them helped the other and their love for each other and for other people showed in everything they did.

Once in a blue moon, I wrote Mom and encouraged her to try to get Dad back; I told her maybe we three could try again. It seemed to cheer her up. Dad's phone calls, which were pretty rare, were not so encouraging. He seemed happy with his other woman and even talked about marrying her. I could never think of much to say to him, except "How are you?"

The day of the fair arrived. We loaded the pig on the truck and put in Aunt Bessie's prize pies, preserves, and pickles. I felt sorry that I had nothing, but they both assured me that part of me was in their preparations: I had picked the corn for both preserves and pig, and had helped with the pies and pickles. Part of the prizes, if any, would belong to me.

Right after we arrived at the fairgrounds, we fell in with some neighbors—the Gelmis family. They had a daughter, Chastity, and Aunt Bessie and Uncle Carl insisted I see the sights with her. "You'll have more fun with someone your own age," they said.

I wasn't so sure. Chastity was a thin, intense-looking girl, about a year older than I was, and she had a sour expression on her face. But I went along with her because I could see it would make everyone else happy. I was already learning to consider other people's feelings, and that was some accomplishment on my road to a different life.

When Chastity and I started off, I chattered on about Aunt Bessie's preserves and Uncle Carl's pig and the rest of the contestants, but I didn't get much response.

"I heard you were a runaway," Chastity finally said. "Ever get into the occult on any of your trips?"

"The occult?"

"You know—witchcraft, demonology, and that sort of stuff."

"No, I didn't," I replied.

"Well, surely you've heard of witchcraft?" she said, and she sounded exasperated.

"Yes, I guess so, but mostly in school—like burning witches in Salem way back," I replied.

"Well, I'm trying for the third level of witchcraft," she said importantly.

"What's that?" I asked. We were passing a homemade ice cream counter, so I suggested we stop.

While we were eating, Chastity explained to me that the occult was becoming very popular in the United States and that her father was interested in it. "He's not really in it the way I am, though," she said. "He just reads about it. I practice it. Why, I've even talked to Satan, and he's talked to me."

"You have?" I was bewildered; this was all new to me. I decided to start at the beginning. "What's the third level of witchcraft?"

Chastity's face lit up and her eyes burned with an inner fire as she explained that the first step is to learn and understand the concept of witchcraft through study; the second is to instruct two others in the same concepts— "sort of like a chain letter," she explained. After that you formed a "coven" of witches and when you reached the third level you received a golden key from the "prince."

"And that isn't all," she said. "I've seen demons and a lot of other strange things."

"Well, that's very interesting," I said, "but how do you talk to Satan?"

"I did, but only once, and it worked. I got a boy to talk to me in school by asking Satan to help me."

The more Chastity talked, the more uncomfortable I became. I didn't believe in any of these things, but then, I wasn't sure, either. I wished for the comfortable presence of Uncle Carl or Aunt Bessie, or better still, both of them.

We had finished eating, so I said to Chastity, "Come on, we'd better go see some of the things at the fair."

"Don't you want to join my coven?" she asked eagerly. "I could instruct you, and—"

"Well, right now I'd better go see if my uncle's pig won the blue ribbon," I said, and walked on ahead. Uncle Carl was standing near the pig-judging and I was never so glad to see anyone in my life! He had lost, but he didn't seem to mind. "Not enough tender, loving care, I guess," he said, and then, spotting me, he laughed and added, "or you didn't give her enough corn!"

I stuck to Uncle Carl and Aunt Bessie like a burr for the rest of the day. There was something evil about Chastity and I was afraid to be alone with her.

At last the long day was over and we headed home. On the way, I told my aunt and uncle about Chastity—from them I was learning to communicate, too. Uncle Carl didn't laugh when I told him. He said he had heard that the Gelmis family was interested in the occult, but if he had realized Chastity was in that deep, he wouldn't have insisted I go with her.

"So long as you live for Jesus, you need not fear witchcraft or any evil powers," he said. "Jesus met the devil in the wilderness and defeated him, and He can break any evil spirit or spell that might try to bind you."

I got kind of scared. Down deep in my heart I knew I wasn't living for Jesus.

Aunt Bessie put her arm around me, and I felt her care for me. "I'm going to tell you something I said I wouldn't," she told me. "But I think it'll make you feel better. Your father called last night and he's coming out to Ohio to see you today; he wants to talk to you." She turned to Uncle Carl. "We're late, Carl; he may already be there," she said.

And he was. The last time I had seen him, his face had been contorted with rage, as he hit me with his belt. Now he had left my mother and was living with another woman. What could we say to each other?

Uncle Carl and Aunt Bessie excused themselves and left us alone on the porch. Neither of us knew what to do. I was half-afraid to even look at him, so I kept my eyes on the floor.

"Becky, I have been thinking of you a lot," he began hesitantly. "But I didn't know what to do or say. The only thing I can think of to say now is that I have asked Christ to come into my heart. I am a different person since I became a real Christian."

I looked up in astonishment; I never thought I'd hear those words from my father! But the minute I looked in his eyes, I knew it was true; he had the same glow as Bill —the look of a genuine Christian who knows love.

I threw my arms around him and began to sob. All the hate and bitterness I had been feeling for years dropped away with the tears and washed out of my life.

"Oh, Daddy," I said, "I love you so much. I want to make up to you for all the grief and trouble I've caused you. I think I am finally beginning to understand the love of Jesus."

"It's the other way round," Dad said. "But we have one other important person to think about—your mother. You and I have done some terrible things to her and we need to ask her forgiveness—I, much more than you, for you are only a child."

"What about this other women?" I blurted out.

"That is one of the things I need to talk to her about," he said gravely. "I am living alone now and want nothing more than for us to be a family again."

Uncle Carl and Aunt Bessie walked out onto the porch. "How about a bite to eat?" Aunt Bessie asked.

That sounded good; I was starved, whether from the physical exercise at the fair or the emotional strain from meeting with Dad was hard to say. All I knew was that I was hungry!

As usual, it was a delicious meal. Afterwards, Uncle Carl turned to me. "Becky, how would you like to receive Jesus into your heart—as your father did?"

"Oh, I want it in the worst way," I said and I did. "But I don't know how to go about it."

Uncle Carl rose and got his Bible and sat down next to me. He read Scriptures in the Bible that showed me how I had sinned. Then he told me that by asking Jesus to forgive me my sins and by inviting Him into my heart I could be saved, and Christ would live in my life and give me the power to be what God wanted me to be. I would always have the vast resources of Christ's love to help me.

Very simply, Uncle Carl led me in prayers. I asked Jesus to forgive my sins, and invited Him to live in my heart forever. I didn't feel a bolt of lightning hit me or anything as dramatic as I had imagined. But there was a feeling of peace that settled over me.

Dad and I left immediately after supper and we drove all night. No one had called Mom to let her know we were coming, so we had no idea what our reception would be. We were pretty beat when we pulled into the driveway, and both of us were a little afraid of our reception.

It was only six o'clock in the morning and we weren't quite sure what to do, but before we had to decide we saw Mom come out on the porch and pick up the paper. I threw caution to the winds and just ran up and threw myself at her. Her arms went around me, and the warm feeling let me know that everything was going to be all right.

In just a moment, Dad followed and somehow managed to clasp both of us in his arms. All three of us were crying as we walked into the living room. We all wound up on the sofa, tightly clutching each other's hands, as though afraid to let go.

All of us started to talk at once, until Dad finally said, "Let's let Mom speak first, Becky."

She told us that after I had left she had gone back to church. She knew that she needed help desperately and that she needed both of us. Once she committed her life to Christ, she said He had sustained her and she had just hung on during the time Dad and I were gone. She told us that she had prayed for both of us constantly, and knew that somehow her prayers would be answered.

Then Dad told us about the man at work who told him about Christ. Actually, he had given his life to Christ during the noon break at the plant.

I started to tell them about Bill, the young Christian people who picked me up, and Aunt Bessie and Uncle Carl, but it all seemed to get mixed up. Finally, Mom suggested we have some breakfast, which I was glad to get.

Mom fixed us a scrumptious breakfast while Dad and I washed the grime of the night away, and when we sat down, we both started to ask Mom's forgiveness. "Dad, will you say grace first?" Mom asked gently. "Then we can go on talking."

Dad and I were both embarrassed that we were back-sliding already, and he asked God to bless our food and thanked Jesus for His intervention in our lives. Then, between mouthfuls, all three of us apologized to each other. We vowed that we would hurt each other no more, and that, as Mom said, "With God's help, we will try to be the persons He wants us to be."

All three of us committed ourselves, solemnly, to this idea. I wish I could say that this story ended happily ever after, but of course it didn't.

We are still together; we still love each other; we still try. But we have our disagreements. Occasionally, we have a fight. A time or two it has reminded me of the not-so-good old days. But we work at it, daily and constantly, individually.

Each of us has learned, individually, to care, consider, and communicate with the others. Dad and I have learned to let Mom know that she is appreciated and that we love her: we tell her so, as well as try to show her, by giving her flowers or a special card. Mom and I have learned to treat Dad like a king in his own home. We treat him the way we would like him to treat us; we tell him we love him. Dad and Mom have learned to talk things out with me, instead of ordering me arbitrarily to do things; they tell me often, as well as show me, that they love me: I know I am wanted.

I don't want to run away anymore, or if I do, fleetingly, I think of the love and affection I'd lose and the grief I'd cause. Dad doesn't run away; he talks everything out with us, even his problems at the office—he says it helps solve them. Mom doesn't nag or talk about divorce anymore. If she starts, she soon talks it out, and if we sympathize and let her know she is loved, the mood is short-lived. I think that we all know that running away won't solve anything. You can't run away from Jesus.

We have all gotten involved in church life. In addition to that, we have family devotions once a week, which Dad leads. We use the Bible as our guide and check the Scriptures for help in everyday problems, as well as in helping our neighbors. Each week we take one part of the Sermon on the Mount and try to put it to practical use.

One of the most difficult tasks was to love our enemy. He was also our neighbor and one of the most ornery guys who ever lived. But one morning, before Dad went to work, he looked out of the window and saw our neighbor changing his flat tire. It was pouring rain, but Dad went out and helped him. You wouldn't believe what a nice guy that ornery neighbor has turned out to be!

One evening we had the pastor and his family over for dinner. Of course, Dad and I knew that *he* knew about both of us, since Mom had shared her burden with him. We didn't knew how he would receive us, but the whole family was delighted that we were a reunited family in Christ. We talked about many things that night, among them, my past life.

Pastor Hunter said something I'll never forget: "Don't ever forget, Becky," he told me, "that Jesus said that the measure you give is the same measure you receive."

I think about that often, especially when I remember Art and San Francisco; Martha and the East Village; Ned and Hank—yes, I can think of them now and forgive them; Florida and the drunken orgies; and especially poor, rich Nora from Alabama. Communication, care, consideration, and most important—trying to follow Christ's way —are making us a family as we never were before. I know what a home is at last, and we are making ours a part of heaven, instead of a living hell.

Some good things are happening at The Walter Hoving Home.

Dramatic and beautiful changes have been taking place in the lives of many girls since the Home began in 1967. Ninety-four percent of the graduates who have come with problems such as narcotic addiction, alcoholism and delinquency have found release and happiness in a new way of living—with Christ. The continued success of this work is made possible through contributions from individuals who are concerned about helping a girl gain freedom from enslaving habits. Will you join with us in this work by sending a check?

The Walter Hoving Home
Box 194
Garrison, New York 10524
(914) 424-3674

Your Gifts Are Tax Deductible

The Walter Hoving Home.

Keep the Hot Line Hot

Every Christian has a hot line direct to the Father. Whether our Christian walk leaps briskly forward or grinds to a halt depends on whether we make proper use of the privilege of prayer. Some of the foremost Christian writers of our day specifically address themselves to this vital concern. Their experience and insight is yours for the reading.

_____ **ALL THINGS ARE POSSIBLE THROUGH PRAYER by Charles L. Allen**—Practical answers to universal questions about prayer. $1.25 each.

_____ **ADVENTURES IN PRAYER by Catherine Marshall**—Incidents from the authors own life and the lives of others illustrate what an exciting adventure true prayer is. $1.75 each.

_____ **WITH CHRIST IN THE SCHOOL OF PRAYER by Andrew Murray**—One of the worlds devotional classics, designed to teach the privilege and power of prayer. $1.25 each.

_____ **SHAPING HISTORY THROUGH PRAYER AND FASTING by Derek Prince**—How prayer and fasting can influence the course of national and international affairs. $1.25 each.

_____ **MR. JONES, MEET THE MASTER by Peter Marshall**—Sermons and prayers of Peter Marshall as edited by his wife Catherine. $1.50 each.

_____ **GETTING THROUGH TO THE WONDERFUL YOU by Charlie Shedd**—An inspiring answer to the practice of transcendental meditation which offers Christians a viable alternative in prayer. $1.50 each.

_____ **HUNGRY FOR GOD by Ralph Martin**—Stirring personal witness to the transforming power of prayer in everyday life. $1.50 each.

_____ **HOW TO PRAY by R. A. Torrey**—The classic Christian answer to how, when, and where to pray. $1.25 each.

Order From Your Bookstore
If your bookstore does not stock these books. return this Order Form to:
Spire Books, Box 150, Old Tappan, New Jersey 07675
Enclosed is my payment plus $.35 mailing charge on first book ordered, $.10 each additional book.

NAME_____

STREET_____

CITY_____ STATE_____ ZIP_____

_____ amount enclosed ____cash ____ check